DATE		

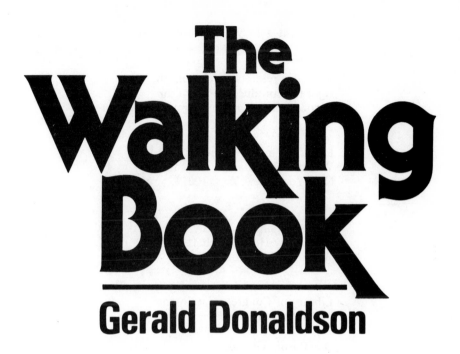

The Walking Book

Gerald Donaldson

A Jonathan-James Book

Holt, Rinehart and Winston
New York

Published by Holt, Rinehart and
Winston, 383 Madison Avenue,
New York, New York 10017.

Published simultaneously in
Canada by Holt, Rinehart and
Winston of Canada, Limited.

Library of Congress Cataloging
in Publication Data

Donaldson, Gerald.
  The walking book.

    "A Jonathan-James book."
    Bibliography: p.175
    1. Walking. 2. Walking — Physiological aspects.
I. Title.
GV199.5.D66   796.5'1   78-14161
ISBN Hardbound: 0-03-049361-7
ISBN Paperback: 0-03-049356-0

First Edition

Printed in the United States of America
10 9 8 7 6 5 4 3 2 1

"Give me thy hand, stand up:
Prithee, let's walk."

William Shakespeare

CONTENTS

Foreword

Our future lies at our feet.

About a million years ago one of our ancestors rose up on to his hind legs and took the first hesitant step towards civilization. Our ability to walk is the primary reason we have come as far as we have.

Walking was born with man and the reverse is true. Until those first steps were taken we were just another animal. But our ability to move about on our own two feet enabled us to leave behind the lower forms of life.

We have come a long way but we have paid a high price. Our bodies have been left behind in the race for progress. Technology rules but shares the throne with obesity. Our stomachs sag, our hearts ache (and often stop), our muscles wither, and we grow old before our time.

For most of the long and rocky road into the twentieth century the very act of survival demanded energy to be expended and our bodies thrived on the effort. But now we have tamed the environment and simplified our lives to the point that most of us must seek other means of keeping our mental and physical selves in tune.

A great deal of contemporary thought and theory is devoted to improving the state of our minds and bodies through exercise. In the name of fitness we are asked to jog, run, jump through hoops, sweat, and stand on our heads. But the oldest, easiest, and most natural way to well-being has been overlooked. It lies right at our feet in the lost art and pleasure of walking.

CHAPTER ONE

"The age is dull and mean. Men
creep, not walk."
John Whittier

1.

A Brisk Walk Through a Million Years

We got here on foot, but the return trip will be much faster. We are asleep behind the wheel of technology.

To begin to appreciate the importance of walking in getting us to where we now stand, we need to look back over our shoulders whence we came and retrace the steps taken by early man.

There we were a million years ago, groveling about on all fours in the primordial slime with everything else. But for some reason we had been formed with a skeletal structure in the legs and feet

If we stop walking those whom we left behind might conceivably catch up.

5

that gave us the capability to begin to stand erect. One day some far-sighted simian made use of this to climb up into a tree. Here we swung about in grand style for a few millennia.

Then we came back down to earth and knuckle-walked along through time. The more we walked, the more we changed. Legs lengthened, arms shortened, and our pelvis became wide enough to hold our torso erect above our legs. It took thousands of years but the more upright we stood, the further we traveled out of the swamps. We became a hominid — a manlike creature.

The greatest contribution of walking to mankind is the ability it gave us to become *homo sapiens* or "knowing man". As soon as our hands were freed from the task of walking they could be used in other endeavors. The hands made weapons and tools. They became skillful and our pea-sized brains grew and blossomed with the effort of thinking up new ways to employ them. Meanwhile we walked further afield, out of the tropical woodland savanna environment to the mountains, prairies, desert, and tundra. The world was at our feet.

As walkers we became king of the beasts. We could outsmart our food. The ever-widening ranges of the hunt moved us into new encounters that forced us to develop different skills and attitudes. We could walk away from nasty situations and dream up better ones, using the experience of the past to provide for the future. Our feet carried out our desires for exploration, discovery, and the pursuit of knowledge.

About thirty-five thousand years ago we stopped slugging it out toe-to-toe with nature. Man the walker had arrived. Newly won locomotive capabilities helped us to master and shape our environment. Walking distances determined the location, shape, and size of the first primitive encampments. They had to be no more than a quick walk away from danger and near edible plants, water, and hunting grounds. The scope and development of these first pockets of civilization were limited to a ten to fifteen mile radius — the distance one could walk and return during the daylight hours.

The stronger walkers ruled the roost. They were the more accomplished hunters and providers. Because they walked more, their strength increased, they became more aggressive, and their wits sharpened. The better walkers became the first ruling class. They were respected and served by their less mobile fellows. Because the hunt was all important, it became a central theme of early religious cults and walkers were worshiped.

And so it came to pass that the walkers inherited the earth. Societies were shaped and history written by our pedestrian predecessors. Civilization took great strides forward when the religion-oriented monarchies in Egypt and Greece organized people into city states. Agriculture was developed and animals domesticated to provide more reliable sources of food. Hunting was no longer as important. Walkers became workers to serve the common good, or slaves or soldiers to serve and protect the ruling class, who — being in charge — no longer needed to walk.

But the feet that had transported our ancestors this far now carried them off in other directions. Philosophers, thinkers, poets, artists, and dreamers took to their feet to unleash their minds. The concept of art and the appreciation of its beauty began with the human anatomy. Painting and sculpture attempted to capture its perfect proportions.

The first great cities of the world were built to

Thinking man made great strides forward in ancient cities such as Athens, built on a human scale.

serve pedestrian man and inspire him with social and religious cohesiveness. Architecture was designed on a human scale for people on foot. The arrangement of the buildings and monuments such as the Acropolis was based on lines of sight so that they could be admired from any angle, no matter where one stood.

Although the wheels of progress began to turn more quickly, they were not allowed to run over walkers. Julius Caesar forbade heavy wagons within the central city after dusk. The Forum of Pompeii was laid out as an exclusive precinct for pedestrians. The *Talmud*, the Hebraic book of laws, decreed that special areas should be set aside along main thoroughfares where footsore people could unload their burdens and cool their heels. These areas were to be clearly marked and separated from vehicular intrusion by a perimeter of metal spikes or stone bollards.

The Roman legionary walked twenty-one miles a day.

Long after animals were harnessed to provide transport, society's leaders still relied on footpower to extend their influence and control their empires. The Roman legionary, walking twenty-one miles a day, marched up and down the length and breadth of Europe, Britain, North Africa, and the Middle East to conquer them for the Caesars in their chariots. Eventually the sedentary Caesars, spoiled by the good life and undoubtedly less fit, were overthrown and trampled underfoot by those whom they had oppressed.

As the years rolled by our debt to our feet increased. The great migrations were made on foot. Walkers set out to improve their lot in life, and frequently to rape and pillage. They plodded relentlessly across the face of the earth, advancing at the pace of the slowest among them — the old folk with the wisdom of the past and the children with the promise for the future. Some of their leaders rode or sailed on ahead but it was those who followed on foot who took possession of the land and sowed the seeds of civilization.

In medieval times the pedestrian was king of the road. Planners built cities around a central plaza where people could mill about at will. This was the market place, the location for festivals, public pronouncements, great occasions, and everyday socializing for those on foot.

Walking became the way to adventure. While the knights, encumbered by their shining armor, had to ride on their spirited chargers, thousands of foot soldiers tramped along behind on the Crusades. Hordes of pilgrims made tracks to religious shrines through all the countries of Europe and the Middle and Far East. Young men set off to seek their fortunes. Wandering minstrels, troubadors, scholars, poets, writers, jugglers, and acrobats took to the open road, spreading culture far and wide.

Leonardo da Vinci was a champion of pedestrianism.

Leonardo da Vinci, a great walker himself, planned a city with elevated streets for pedestrians to isolate them from the cut and thrust of cart traffic. The old city of Bologna has a twenty mile network of covered sidewalks for cool, dry walking in summer and a snow-free way in winter. Da Vinci was a champion of walkers in other ways, making extensive anatomical studies of human locomotion and designing buildings on a human scale.

The centuries of fancy footwork left indelible imprints wherever walkers went. The British system of linear measurement is based on the foot. A yard was the distance of an average pace. "Mile" comes from the Latin *mille*, or thousand. The Roman mile was one thousand paces. The word "walk" as we know it came into being around 1000 A.D. by way of "wealcian" which meant "to roll or toss" in Old English, then "to move about or travel" in Middle English. To get from "wealcian" to "walk" we incorporated bits of the Middle Dutch and German "walken" meaning "to knead, beat, or press".

Then suddenly about two hundred years ago walking as a way of life stopped short and we have gone downhill ever since. The wheel took over our lives. Public coaches began to travel the roads, then came trains, planes, and a car in every driveway. The wheel of progress whirled around like an enormous eraser, rubbing out a million years of footloose freedom. When the world of walking came apart at the seams, so did we. Arches fell, bodies bulged, tensions gripped us, our hearts failed us, and we

The walker's worst enemy.

became physical wrecks. Sloth set in.

So we have come full circle. We find ourselves right back where we started, floundering around in the swamps of the unfit and looking for a way out. We need look no further than our feet.

Man is still the only mammal that habitually walks upright. The desire to place one foot in front of the other and move is still strong within us. Mobility is the first thing we want to achieve as babies and the last thing we want to give up before we die. In between those times is where we fall down. For most of us walking is confined to the few short steps it takes to travel between bed, the refrigerator, the car, and the television set.

All those years that we walked around on earth we wanted to get to the moon. It is significant that when we finally got there our first steps on the lunar landscape were commemorated by these words: "That's one small step for man, one giant leap for mankind."

It is high time that we came back down to earth and took a whole series of steps forward for the good of our bodies, minds, and mankind. Happily for us all the easiest, most painless way to do it is to take the million year old cure.

CHAPTER TWO

"Some thinke their feete be where
their head shall never come."
John Davies

2

The Anatomy of Walking

**An intimate examination of the human loco-
motive mechanism and a tribute to the physical
achievement of walking.**

It is often said that walking is as natural as
breathing. We are born breathing and a few months
later we begin to take our first steps. But like
breathing and the other functions of the body,
walking is a complicated process involving much
more than merely placing one foot in front of the
other. We have to crawl before we can walk.

*Our two hundred and
six bones have
evolved for walking
upright.*

Walking is the reason we look and move the way
we do. The human anatomy evolved into its present
shape because of that momentous decision by our
primitive ancestors to get up and go. An adult
skeleton is a tower of two hundred and six bones that
have adapted to our unique posture. When you
consider that one quarter of those bones — fifty-two
in all — are located in the feet, it is easier to
comprehend the importance of walking to what
makes us tick.

At last count there were more than sixty trillion
cells in the body. So tiny that millions of them may
be found in a half inch cube of human tissue, they
combine to form the muscles, blood, nerves, bone,
and the internal and external tissue that support
them. To operate efficiently they need food to
provide raw material for the release of energy,
oxygen to help break down the food, and water to
help transport it. A very large proportion of these
cells exist for the purpose of moving us about. When
all of them are functioning as they should, the system
is unbeatable.

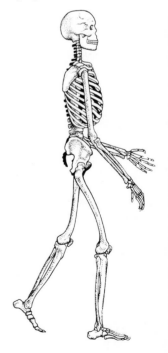

13

The bones

The spine is the backbone of our walking mechanism. Babies are born with a straight one; as soon as they graduate from crawling it takes on an S-shaped appearance and performs like a double-curved spring. In the act of walking the twenty-six articulated vertebrae yield and spring back with each stride.

The lower spine slots neatly into the pelvic girdle. Fitting into the front of the pelvic girdle at each side is the femur, the largest bone in the body, usually about twenty inches long. It is also the strongest. When a one hundred and twenty-five pound woman goes for a walk, her femur or thigh bone must withstand a pressure of twelve hundred pounds per square inch at certain stress points.

The femur, which carries our body weight to the tibia and fibula, is joined to them at the knee. The tibia or shinbone is the larger; the fibula is a long slender bone attached above and below to the side of the tibia.

Then come the feet, the basic foundation of the whole body. They are cunningly arranged so that the twenty-six bones in each one distribute our body weight evenly over three main points: the base of the big toe, the base of the little toe, and the heel. Longitudinal and transverse arches are located within these three points. Maximum support of the total skeletal structure is maintained only when the body weight is balanced over the arches and the feet remain relatively parallel.

Our bones have to be as strong as iron girders. And they are, but not nearly as heavy. In a one hundred and sixty pound man their total weight is only about twenty-nine pounds. Steel bars of comparable size would weigh at least five times as much. Bones are light because they are porous and, in the case of the femur and tibula, of hollow tube construction.

The secret of our bones' strength is in their composition. About one half of their weight is made up of inorganic compounds of calcium, phosphorus, and other minerals. One quarter of their composition is a type of protein fiber called collagen, from the Greek words *kolla* — glue and *gene* — forming. For some unknown reason the remaining quarter of our bone weight is made up of water, but the minerals and the secret ingredient collagen are cemented together to produce great rigidity.

"The footbone connected to the ankle bone, the ankle bone connected to the leg bone, the leg bone connected to the hip bone, them bones, them bones, them dry bones" — all of them that move when we walk are linked by ligaments (bands of elastic, fibrous tissue) and fitted together at joints that are flexible. These joints are lined with cartilage, a glassy-smooth tissue that reduces friction, and lubricated by synovial fluid, a secretion of watery consistency that acts as "joint oil". The biggest joint of them all is where the leg bone connects to the hip bone. Here the rounded ball end of the femur is held in a fist-like grip by the pelvic girdle that enables a walker to stride along in "seven league boots".

The muscles

To get the bones in our body to move requires muscles. Every one of us has approximately six hundred and fifty of them whose pull on the bones makes motion possible. The skeletal muscles, attached to bone by bands of tissue called tendons, act like cables to pull the bones where we want them to go.

When we walk the solid shafts of bone in our legs are pulled into motion by the contraction of the muscles surrounding them. They work in pairs — one muscle, a flexor, contracting to pull a bone forward and another muscle, an extensor, contracting to pull it back. In the case of the knee the flexor muscles bend the hinge joint and the extensors straighten it again.

Most of the muscles in the lower body have names as complicated as the tasks they perform are remarkable. *Gluteus maximus, iliotibial band, vastus lateralis, semimembranosis, gastrocnemius, biceps femoris, soleus* and *vastus medialis* all help us to walk. The *sartorius*, the Latin word for tailor, is the longest muscle in the body. It was given this name because it comes into play in the cross-

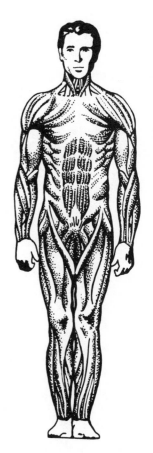

Most of our six hundred and fifty muscles are involved in walking.

15

legged position which tailors traditionally assumed. In the thigh *sartorius* and four bundles of muscles on each side of it, called the quadriceps, not only move the legs but help us maintain our balance.

Whether we are muscle-bound or not, *sartorius* and the others are as strong as a horse and able to support one thousand times their own weight. In the old days our hard-working forefathers used to average some nineteen thousand steps a day — about seven miles. This meant that their muscles did an amount of daily work equivalent to lifting dozens of tons of grain on to a wagon four feet high.

Our bones and muscles live on blood. It provides them with the food and oxygen that combine in the cells to produce energy. The most important muscle in the body pumps blood out to our extremities through some sixty thousand miles of tubing. The heart, about the size of a fist and weighing about a pound or so, pushes the ten pints of blood in the average adult body through more than one thousand complete cycles of the circulatory system each day. Just to keep us alive it does enough work in twenty-four hours equivalent to lifting the body one mile straight up. But it thrives on work. Like all our muscles, its state of health depends on how much work we give it to do. If a muscle is not used it tends to shrink and waste away.

The chemistry, senses, and physics

Some amazing things happen when we tell our feet to take a walk. From the brain, the headquarters of our nervous system, the message whizzes along at a speed of two hundred to three hundred and fifty feet per second, down through the spinal column to motor nerves in our muscles. On arrival this signal triggers a series of chemical changes in the muscles, causing them to contract and provide the energy necessary to move our feet. What happens next is not yet fully understood.

This much is known. The muscle membrane is put on the alert by a substance called acetylcholine which acts as a stimulant. The actual energy which contracts the muscle is supplied by the breakdown of another chemical, adenosine triphosphate. This in turn is made possible by the conversion of glycogen, a complex sugar stored in the muscle as a source of fuel and which is supplied to the blood in the form of glucose, another sugar. The muscle contraction is then touched off by the release of calcium from the small sacs within muscle membrane. It is thought that the muscle is allowed to relax after a certain amount of calcium has been brought back and stored in these sacs.

All of this complicated chemical activity takes place within split seconds. Nothing that technology has yet devised comes close to matching this miraculous performance. Those scientists who are studying it have calculated that an electronic computer, to duplicate the efforts of our three pound brain in coordinating its traffic messages, would occupy a space as big as a giant skyscraper.

Before we can walk about skillfully in our environment we must develop two important senses — a sense of balance and muscle sense. The organs of balance are little fluid-filled structures in the inner ear. Waving in the fluid are hairs which, pulled by the movements of the head and by the force of gravity, tell the brain which way we are moving and which way is up. Thus oriented to the ground, we use our muscle sense to evaluate messages sent from tiny nerve endings in our skin, muscles, and joints which tell the brain where each movable part of the body is at any given time. Even the most leisurely stroll calls for a smooth coordination of muscle sense with balance, sight, and touch. The eyes give us a point of reference to help keep the movement of walking in perspective. (To discover the importance of the eyes in maintaining a sense of balance, try standing on one leg with your eyes closed.) As babies we need a lot of training and practice to put all of this together into a walk.

With a body so wonderfully equipped for walking it might seem a simple matter of just hopping to it, striking out on our own two feet in all directions and conquering all that we encounter. Not so. First our bodies must engage in combat with, sometimes defy, and often take advantage of several laws of physics.

When we stand the force of gravity pulls our body

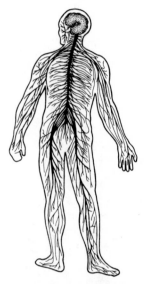

Locomotive messages from the brain travel at speeds up to three hundred and fifty feet per second.

downward toward the center of the earth. Our center of gravity is usually located at between fifty-five and fifty-seven percent of our total height from the ground, which places it in the region of the hips on most people. Because a body is balanced when its center of gravity is over its supporting base (the feet), we can maintain our equilibrium relatively easily when standing still. But as soon as we take a step, we are off balance, and ready to be pulled down by gravity. Thus walking involves a continuous loss and recovery of balance.

Throughout the act of walking we have to contend with the laws of Sir Isaac Newton, whose discoveries affect our every movement. Even before we take that first gravity-defying step we must overcome his Law of Inertia: "An object at rest will remain at rest until acted upon by an outside force." This presents a major challenge to walking. Fortunately he provided a solution in the other part of this same law: "An object in motion will remain in motion at the same speed in a straight line until acted upon by an outside force." So with our first step we overcome inertia by the work of our muscles and as long as we keep going, all is well. But if we stop, it requires greater effort to begin moving again.

The discoveries of Sir Isaac Newton affect our every movement.

Then comes his Law of Momentum: "When a body is acted upon by a force, its resulting acceleration is proportional to the force and inversely proportional to the mass." And his Law of Force: "Every force is accompanied by an equal and opposite force."

The walking stride begins with the body swaying forward to overcome its inertia. To keep the body balanced, one of the walker's feet must swing forward to widen the body's pedestal support. The leg still to the rear of the body then provides the propulsive force that drives the body ahead. After the push-off by this rear foot, it also swings forward to strike the ground heel first. This heel strike concludes the swing phase and the body continues to move forward with the weight rolling across the ball of the foot until another push-off is delivered by the rear foot.

In a way we walk as a wheel turns — the rolling

action of the body's center of gravity and the rotary application of propulsive and supportive forces by the legs and feet roll us along. But where we have it all over the wheel is in our ability to experience the sensation of walking.

When we walk we are unconscious of all these sequential movements. The defying of gravity, the series of forward falls caught in the nick of time, and the continuous loss and recovery of balance are done effortlessly. When we hit our stride — with the step length that is exactly right for our body dimensions and a speed that is the product of our very own weight and muscular strength — then something miraculous happens.

There is a sensation of rhythm, a joy in self-motivation, and a pleasure from being at one with nature — moving as we were intended to do. We float along, intoxicated by the exuberance of our own velocity, glorying in our awakened senses, and feeling as free as fish in the sea, birds in the air, and our own fellow creatures on earth.

We are off and walking. All sixty trillion cells are working together in such perfect harmony that the experience can make our heart sing and sweep our spirit off its feet.

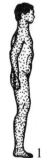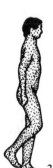

1   2   3   4   5

1. *We stand erect with feet slightly apart to balance our center of gravity.*
2. *Defying gravity, we lean forward to overcome inertia.*
3. *One foot pushes off the ground, which pushes back, and our center of gravity falls forward.*
4. *The leg swings forward in a pendular motion, the foot strikes the ground, and balance is restored.*
5. *The other foot lifts off and the cycle continues with the arms swinging in opposition to the legs.*

CHAPTER THREE

"That man is by no means poor,
who has the use of everything he
wants. If it is well with your belly,
your back, and your feet, regal
wealth can add nothing greater."
Horace

3

The Road to Health

The medicine in our feet, and how each one of us has two doctors: the left leg and the right.

When a doctor is ready to hang out his shingle he takes the *Hippocratic Oath,* embodying the code of medical ethics and named after Hippocrates, the

"Walking is man's best medicine" said Hippocrates.

most celebrated physician of Greek antiquity. This gentleman, generally regarded as the father of medicine, stated flatly: "Walking is man's best medicine." Today a growing number of his successors agree with that proclamation. It is reassuring to know that the medical profession is there to help in time of need, but if we take their advice and walk more and more, we will need them less and less.

Most of us suffer from lack of exercise, the direct cause of many of the aches and pains of the twentieth century. Without a certain minimum level of exercise we become obese, breathless at the slightest exertion, permanently tired, and are more prone to ulcers, diabetes, varicose veins, back aches, muscular tension, arteriosclerosis, heart disease, and a host of rheumatic problems. The list of hypokinetic diseases (the whole spectrum of inactivity-induced physical and mental derangements) grows by leaps and bounds. If one of them doesn't attack us first, there is a distinct possibility that premature aging, often a by-product of lack of exercise, will overtake and pass us by. Hippocrates, in his wisdom, described why this is so: "That which is used develops. That which is not used wastes away." In *The Beautiful People's Beauty Book,* the lovely Princess Luciana Pignatelli echoed that sentiment: "A body that cannot move and bend freely, no matter how slender and pampered, no longer looks young."

The medicine of walking

Should we fall victim to any of these disorders it is often possible to help cure them through exercise. New evidence of the therapeutic powers of moving the body in the way it is built to do emerges almost daily, and more and more doctors are prescribing the treatment that lies at our feet. As well as being an indispensable conditioner for the healthy, exercise is a valuable cure for the sick. And what Thomas Jefferson said in 1776 holds true today: "Of all exercises walking is the best."

In hospitals, many doctors and surgeons now have their patients walk up and down the corridors as part of their treatment. Post operative patients, too, are urged to take their first steps as soon as possible to prevent blood clots and hasten convalescence through stimulation of the circulatory and digestive systems. A normally active person who becomes bed-ridden loses up to eighty percent of his or her physical condition after one month. Walking also helps an ill person's morale by awakening dulled senses. The act of walking embodies life itself.

In or out of hospitals, digestion and functioning of the kidneys and bowels are aided by walking because the regular mobility of the locomotive system promotes the same in the digestive system. If everyone walked as they should, the crutch of laxatives might well be thrown away. The Jewish physician, Maimonides, who practiced in a suburb of Cairo during the twelfth century, alluded to this: "A person should walk prior to the meal until his body begins to be warmed . . . Anyone who lives a sedentary life and does not exercise . . . even if he eats good foods and takes care of himself according to proper medical principles — all his days will be painful ones and his strength shall wane." Two hundred years later the Dutch humanist, Erasmus, supported Maimonides with: "Before supper walk a little; after supper do the same." Finally, former American president, Harry S. Truman, offered his prescription on how to live to be eighty: "Take a two mile walk every morning before breakfast."

People with broken bones in the lower limbs are supplied with walking casts whenever possible. Studies have shown that those parts of the body immobilized in plaster casts lose thirty percent of their muscular strength within one week. Bones that are walked demineralize at a lesser rate and thus are less likely to break in the first place. When broken, exercise is essential for the mending process.

Nicotine addicts can take heart from the curative powers of walking which help offset the damaging effects of their habit by cleaning out the circulatory and respiratory systems. As well, there is nothing like a brisk walk to underscore the negative aspects of smoking on the lungs and, at the very least, people are less likely to smoke when moving. For this

Thomas Jefferson said: "Of all exercises walking is the best."

reason many chest specialists recommend that heavy smokers cut down by walking away from their problem.

Even those lungs that have never known a puff of smoke can benefit from walking, which increases their air capacity and causes breathing to be deeper, smoother, and less frequent. This occurs because the muscles of respiration are made stronger through walking. The exercise also increases the number of capillaries in the lung tissue which leads to more efficient extraction of oxygen from the air breathed in. All of these benefits help decrease shortness of breath and improve respiratory recovery rates.

Walking is a relatively new treatment for heart attack victims. It has been found that a damaged heart when exercised will often help repair itself by growing new capillaries and sprouting new artery branches. These may bypass the damaged area and take over the job of the narrowed or blocked arteries. Patients begin a walking program, sometimes as soon as six weeks after an attack, by taking a few steps at a leisurely pace, and gradually building up to three and a half miles an hour over longer distances.

Angina, caused by insufficient blood supply to the heart, responds well to walking. At the University of California Dr. A.A. Kattus and his associates studied the effects of walking on fifty people with this ever-increasing problem. Supported by drugs to treat their angina, they began a daily walking routine which for some was just a few hundred feet and for others up to two miles each day. In many cases new bridges of circulation were found to have developed around the offending areas and in a few patients all evidence of angina disappeared. A total of seventy-five percent of those treated in this way showed a marked improvement in their condition.

Walking may help the bored and the boring. Our central nervous system — the one through which we perceive the world by sight, sound, smell, taste, and touch — performs below par without exercise. To walk is to heighten all these senses because each of them depends on movement to operate optimally. The impulses generated in the muscles during walking stimulate eyes, ears, nose, mouth, and the entire surface of the skin with the result that life takes on a new and vital perspective when it is walked through.

"Nerves" of another kind, those subject to stress, can be strengthened and soothed by walking. Dr. Hans Selye, the world's foremost authority on stress, proved the anti-stress value of walking with the help of twenty laboratory rats. In his experiment, conducted at the University of Montreal, Dr. Selye subjected ten of the rats to a month long program of electric shocks, blinding lights, and loud noises. At the end of the month all ten of the unfortunate creatures were dead. The remaining ten rats were walked on treadmills until they were in prime condition, then given exactly the same stress program as those that had died. At the end of one month all ten of the rats who had walked remained alive and reasonably well, if perhaps somewhat disoriented. It seems that the action of walking had helped them withstand stress. Another experiment, this time with sheep at Cornell University, showed how walking can be an antidote to stress. Psychologists used ringing bells and electric shocks to make a flock of sheep apprehensive. In a short time they exhibited signs of mental disturbance, became listless, and lost interest in food. When the sheep were given relief from the bells and shocks for a minimum of two hours a day, their symptoms of stress disappeared and they resumed the habits of sheep. For human beings, too, a two hour walk is one of the best ways to counteract a stressful day. Regular intervals of walking help develop greater resistance to, tolerance of, and quicker recovery from both mental and physical fatigue and stress.

In his book, *The Habits of Health*, Dr. Donald Norfolk tells how chronic stress leads to tension: "With our noses to the grindstone and our shoulders to the wheel, we are constantly striving to climb the ladder of success, grasping to take hold of a bigger share of the world's material wealth, or sometimes merely fighting to keep our heads above water. Each image conveys a state of tense, earnest struggle." Dr. Norfolk calls tension "a bad neuromuscular habit"

Few signs of stress can be found on a country walk.

27

in which muscles tighten, blood pressure soars, and "stress hormones are poured out into the circulation as the metabolic engines race." The resulting breathlessness, heart palpitations, and other alarming psychosomatic indications cause further anxieties which disturb sleep and bring on frowns, wrinkles, stiff necks, headaches, and more. The antidote for tension is relaxation. Relaxation, for some, comes in bottles of pills and alcohol but it is also available in pure, undiluted, natural form in our feet. Walking helps promote progressive relaxation and releases muscular tension. Shakespeare said it in Act III of his play, *Cymbeline:* "A turn or two I'll walk, to still my beating mind."

It has been estimated that fully sixty percent of back pain stems from muscle weakness and fatigue brought on by inactivity. In an active body the internal pressure of the muscles in the abdominal wall plays a supporting role to the spine. In an unwalked body these muscles sag and fall down on the job, forcing the spine to take up the slack. The spine reacts by aching in its lower regions. A walking program helps relieve the pain and builds up the muscles so that they can support the spine as intended. Walking increases overall muscular strength, endurance, and tone which leads to proper alignment of the complete skeleton and all of the internal organs.

Walking improves the way we look as well as the way we feel. Muscles that are strengthened and toned by walking are smoother and more streamlined without being large or hypertrophied as in the case of weight-lifters. Healthy muscles help maintain good posture which is an excellent preventive measure for double chins, sagging abdomens, and rounded shoulders. The development of an efficient and graceful walk helps promote overall balance, timing, and rhythm. Even the most clumsy, non-athletic individual can develop physical grace by walking more and doing it properly. Finally, well-walked muscles are less susceptible to their own aches and pains. Shakespeare put words to this effect in the mouth of Henry VIII: "We'll walk awhile and ease our legs," (though Henry was not

Henry VIII suffered from the effects of not walking enough.

much of a walker and looked the part).

The combined effect of all these benefits obtainable through walking is to reduce the degenerative consequences of aging. The eminent Russian physiologist, Pavlov, maintained that everyone could live to be a hundred; if they didn't it was due to "intemperance, lack of regularity, and their criminal attitude towards their bodies." Presumably Pavlov failed to follow his own advice, for he died in 1916 at sixty-seven (an average age). Had he walked more he might have lasted longer and enjoyed his stay better. Walking plays a major role in the long, productive, and happy lives of the celebrated centenarians living in the Caucasian mountains of Russia. A report from the Georgian Gerontology Center, which has studied them extensively, says: "Their entire lives consist of rationally organized cycles of outdoor work, rest and play." For these people walking is the way of life.

Although chronological age is fixed, physiological age has a variable of thirty years. We cannot ignore our birthdays but it is possible for a sixty-five year old person to have the appearance and agility of a thirty-five year old. Regular walking helps bring about this transformation by combating the onset of infirmity, feebleness, frailness, low energy, and loss of the fight against gravity that typify the older and unexercised body. The best way to get to the fountain of youth may be to walk.

If the positive powers of walking follow through to the very end of a lifetime, it now appears that they begin at the actual moment of birth. A current study in England shows that walking improves the quality of entry into the world. This report in the *British Medical Journal* concludes that: "The advantages to the mother and her fetus indicate that ambulation (walking) in labor should be encouraged." Researchers at the Birmingham Maternity Hospital had thirty-four pregnant women walk around prior to giving birth, while thirty-four others remained in bed. The walking mothers were monitored for fetal heart rate and uterine contractions by radiotelemetry. For them, labor was several hours shorter and they required less pain-relieving medication than those who remained in the traditional prone position. In fact twenty of the thirty-four walkers required no drugs whatsoever. Thirty-one of the ambulatory women had completely unassisted deliveries, while twelve of those kept in bed required assistance.

CHAPTER FOUR

"Two hands upon the breast,
And labour's done;
Two pale feet crossed in rest,
The race is won."
Dinah Craik

4

The Steps to Fitness

How to walk the heart into shape, walking versus fat, and how walking compares with other exercise.

All those people jogging and running up and down the length and breadth of the land are chasing after physical fitness. Along the way they may branch out in other directions and pant down paths in search of fulfillment, peace, self-esteem and such, but their primary goal is to get the exercise necessary to make them fit. In bygone times the very act of living gave us enough exercise to be fit; now most of us must find it in other ways. Fortunately the technology that created this state of affairs has bequeathed to us the leisure time to regain what we have lost. And we don't have to run after it. We can walk.

When we are physically fit we are able to use the maximum physical potential of our body, and all of its parts are operating at their optimal functional capacity. If a body cannot do what it is built to do, then that body is not fit. Fitness has little to do with specific athletic skills, although athletics can certainly help to develop and maintain fitness. The way to create and keep fitness in a body is to use it in the way for which it was intended. We are constructed for activity and regular activity is essential for maximum body function and health.

In his book, *Dr. Sheehan on Running,* George Sheehan, M.D. observes: "If God had meant us to walk, He would have given us feet. He would have given us a sport for these ordinary G.I. (God-issued) feet — a sport for rich and poor, for old and young

Homer praised the cerebral satisfaction of walking.

and for either sex; a sport free from injury and interruption; a sport with physical exertion and mental relaxation; a sport that would not penalize ineptitude, but would reward excellence; a sport that is as natural as, for instance, walking."

Physical fitness is comprised of many components and variables, often related in complex ways not yet fully understood. Part of being fit is to have a pervasive feeling of well-being that is compounded of physical, mental, and social factors. Fitness brings on an aura of elation similar to what Homer described in Book XIII of his works, so that we "seem to walk on wings, and tread on air." But there is more to it than cerebral satisfaction. After all an intoxicated person often has a feeling of well-being but is not necessarily fit.

To measure real fitness we have to encompass the whole spectrum of variable physiological functions and physical skills. Therefore to be fit means efficiency in muscular strength, power and endurance, speed, agility, coordination, flexibility, recovery, accuracy, balance, alertness, steadiness, timing, rhythm, reaction time, and the proper functioning of the body's digestive, nervous, respiratory, and circulatory systems. As we have seen, the simple act of putting our feet into motion benefits almost every one of those functions and skills.

Though there is almost universal agreement concerning these benefits it is difficult to measure them precisely. In the words of the American College of Sports Medicine: "Although many such variables and their adaptive response to training have been documented, the lack of sufficient in-depth and comparative data relative to frequency, intensity and duration of training make them inadequate to use as comparative models." The ACSM, with headquarters at the University of Wisconsin, has probably studied the subject of fitness more than any other group.

In July 1978 they released a bulletin entitled *Position Statement on the Recommended Quantity and Quality of Exercise for Developing and Maintaining Fitness in Healthy Adults.* In it they indicate that fitness is best achieved and measured by working on two specific exercise-dependent determinants: Aerobic Capacity and Body Composition. Both of these are optimized by endurance-type exercises — that is, by modes of activity that use the body's large muscle groups, that can be maintained continuously, and that are rhythmic and aerobic in nature. This describes walking to a "T".

Aerobic capacity

Aerobic is an adjective meaning living or active only in the presence of oxygen. Aerobic capacity is the term referring to the maximum amount of oxygen that the body is able to use when involved in strenuous exertion. It means more than simply the amount of oxygen breathed in — pulmonary ventilation (also improved by walking) — but rather the maximum quantity that can be transported by the blood to the working cells of the body, and particularly the muscle cells. Here the oxygen is used to burn the fuels — glycogen and fat — which release the energy required for physical work.

As you sit reading this book, providing you are average and non-athletic, you are breathing in an

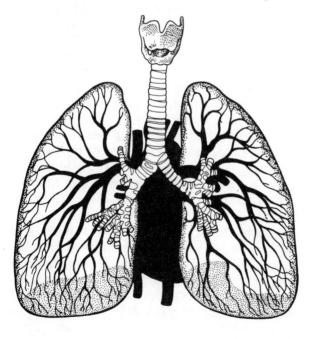

The heart and lungs are the most important beneficiaries of walking.

average of 4.8 liters of air per minute. Of this amount approximately .3 liters of oxygen is picked up by your lungs and transported to your waiting cells. Were you to set the book down and engage in some muscular activity, such as walking briskly upstairs, your cardiovascular (heart/blood vessel) system would extract from 3 to 3.5 liters of oxygen from the up to one hundred liters of air you would inhale in one minute.

One of the objects of exercise is to increase your ability to take in oxygen. Depending on the frequency, intensity, and duration of the exercise it is possible to increase aerobic capacity from five to about twenty-five percent. The greater your aerobic capacity, the better your cardiovascular system operates and vice versa. The key to your cardiovascular system is your heart. Therefore your aerobic capacity is, to a large extent, a measure of the fitness of your heart.

The effects on the heart of an endurance activity like walking are all positive. Your resting heart rate (pulse) will be lower. This lets your heart rest longer between the 100,000 beats it must make every day just to keep you alive. Exercise through walking will increase the stroke volume of the heart, that is the amount of blood pumped with each heartbeat. It will lower the blood pressure and improve the ability of both the heart and blood pressure to recover from strenuous activity. It will make the heart muscle stronger and increase the elasticity of the arteries, which improves the carrying capacity of the capillaries in the heart and in other muscles. An exercised heart can build up a reserve supply of capillaries which are vital in time of high stress on the heart, or in the event of a heart attack. The supply of hemoglobin, the substance in the blood which transports oxygen, is also increased through exercise.

There is another dividend from walking. Every muscle in the body acts as an auxiliary heart, helping to pump blood. When the body is static the blood tends to become stagnant and collect in the lower regions of the extremities. As the body muscles contract in walking, they help pump this blood through the veins back to the heart for reconditioning. This action relieves the heart of full responsibility for circulation and improves the entire circulatory system.

An old Hindu proverb says: "Walking makes for a long life." Much of the truth in this statement concerns the strengthening of the cardiovascular system. Walking helps offset the decline in cardiac capacity that averages about one percent per year in adults after the age of twenty-one. Statistics show that a sedentary sitter is much more likely to have a heart attack than a walker.

Proof positive of the benefits of walking to the heart and its accessories was graphically demonstrated in a study conducted by Michael L. Pollock and others at Wake Forest University in North Carolina. The results were published in the *Journal of Applied Physiology* in January 1971, in a paper entitled "Effects of walking on body composition and cardiovascular function of middle-aged men." Twenty-four men averaging forty-nine years of age were used in this experiment. All of these healthy but sedentary people were tested as they came into the laboratory. Eight of them formed a control group while the remaining sixteen embarked on a walking program. They walked on a treadmill for forty minutes, four times a week for a twenty week period. Their distances progressed from two and a half miles in the first week to three and a quarter miles during weeks sixteen to twenty.

Not surprisingly the non-walking control group showed no changes when tested at the end of the experiment. But the sixteen walkers showed marked improvement in their cardiovascular functions. On average their maximal oxygen intake (aerobic) capacity increased by twenty-eight percent and their pulmonary ventilation (lung capacity) increased by fifteen percent. Their resting heart rate, blood pressure, and heart rate recovery times all decreased dramatically.

Walking for the heart

The American College of Sports Medicine has laid down the basic requirements of fitness training for the improvement of aerobic capacity involving the frequency, duration, and intensity of exercise.

The ACSM's recommended frequency of exercise is from three to five days per week. Walking for pleasure can be enjoyed day in and day out but in brisk walking with fitness as the objective, the days off give the body a better chance to recover and prevent walking for exercise from becoming a chore. Studies have shown the aerobic benefits tend to level out after three to four days of exercise.

The duration of exercise should be from fifteen to sixty minutes of continuous aerobic activity. Naturally the duration depends on the intensity of activity and less time spent walking requires a greater intensity to achieve the same benefits. Obviously less fit people must work at lower intensities and therefore they should walk longer.

A watch and your pulse will give you your heart rate.

The intensity of exercise as recommended by the American College of Sports Medicine should be at between sixty to ninety percent of the maximum heart rate reserve, which equals from fifty to eight-five percent of aerobic capacity. Aerobic capacity is difficult to measure outside a laboratory as maximum heart reserve is arrived at through somewhat complicated mathematics. (Maximum heart reserve is equal to the percentage difference between the resting heart rate and the maximum heart rate, plus the resting heart rate.) What it all means is that younger people should try to walk with their hearts beating at about 130 to 135 beats per minute and older persons should try to achieve a rate of between 110 and 120 beats per minute. These rates approximate the minimum sixty percent of maximum heart rate reserve necessary for improving aerobic capacity.

Heart rate can most easily be found by using a watch and checking the pulse. Simply find the pulse on the thumb side of the wrist or on the neck just to the side of the Adam's apple. Count the beats over a thirty second period and then multiply by two. Normal resting heart rates, which average 60 to 75 beats per minute, are best checked first thing in the morning prior to any activity. To increase the heart rate the required 40 to 60 beats per minute, the intensity of walking activity can be increased by walking faster, walking uphill, up stairs, over rough terrain, or on soft surfaces such as snow or sand. By way of an example, it has been calculated that when a person has a rate of 80 to 90 beats per minute while sitting, walking slowly increases that rate to between 100 and 110 beats per minute. Walking briskly uphill can produce a heart rate of from 130 to 140.

Exercise intensities as measured by heart rate vary with age and level of fitness. Older people have a lower maximum heart rate so their heart rate reserve is lower. It is very important that older and less fit people do not try to walk their heart rate beyond the limits of safety. Prior to walking for fitness everyone, regardless of age, should have a medical examination and get their doctor's advice.

Body composition

Body composition, the second major determinant of fitness as recommended by the American College of Sports Medicine, primarily refers to fat. Physiologists measure total body weight, fat weight, and lean body weight to determine body composition. The relationship between the three determines what percentage of a person's body weight is due to fat.

All indications are that too many of us have undesirable body composition. Obesity is the curse of the western world. In America alone it is estimated that more than seventy million people are overweight. These unfortunates are twice as likely to have symptoms of chronic illness. They are more prone to fatigue, muscular pain, joint pain, headaches, indigestion, constipation, heart disease, diabetes, and kidney problems. Besides looking fat, they are staring early death right in the eye. In fact, a British doctor has calculated that carrying around ten pounds of excess fat is more likely to cause death than smoking twenty-five cigarettes a day.

The fight against fat rages on. People truss, bind, and gag themselves in all manner of anti-fat fads. They embark on countless (and usually futile) diets and they spend fortunes in time and money watching their weight. Better they should contemplate their navels or the mysteries of the universe. Watched

Walkers can have their cake and eat it too without fear of fat.

weight will not waver or shrink. But excess weight that is moved by walking will waste away.

Too much fat is the direct result of sedentary living and is not necessarily caused by overeating. Many obese people eat as little as, or less than slim people. The difference is that the slim burn up a larger proportion of the calories they take in. A kilocalorie is the amount of heat required to raise the temperature of one liter of water to one degree centigrade. Most people refer to them simply as calories. These units are measurements of food energy but for many they are the measurements which represent unwanted pounds and inches.

One pound of human fat is roughly the equivalent of 3500 calories. It matters not what the food source may be, nor whether it is in the form of protein, fats, or carbohydrates. A calorie is a calorie and 3500 of them, taken in without putting some effort out, will result in one pound of extra fat being put on. An apparently harmless looking and good tasting piece of buttered toast with jam constitutes 100 calories. If one were to indulge in this at every breakfast for one year it would create a caloric excess of 36,500 which would weigh in at ten and a half pounds of extra weight. Conversely, if those extra calories were not consumed there would be a similar loss of weight. But, since a continuous aerobic exercise like walking burns off fat, walkers are able to have their toast and eat it too.

Walking for weight loss is often easier and always healthier than the hardships of dieting. Most diets require a radical change of eating habits which people have difficulty maintaining over long periods of time. It is much simpler to develop a new and pleasing habit like walking than it is to break a long-standing one like eating. One can walk — and eat — in peace, comfortable in the knowledge that through this exercise calories can be confronted head on and laid low, rather than having to avoid them in dieting. Another problem of diets is that they may restrict the intake of essential nutrients. (Calories are not all we need from food.) Finally, the emphasis on dieting is often very rapid weight loss, which is unhealthy. For esthetic reasons too, it is better if the body has a chance to adjust slowly to its new shape so that skin doesn't sag. Permanent weight losses tend to be slow weight losses, which is the way it goes with walking.

Excess weight/fat can be lost through types of exercises more strenuous than moderately brisk walking. The problem with these activities is that the unduly fat (and older) people are often not in good enough physical condition to participate in them. Then there is a tendency for enthusiasm to wane and discouragement to set in. At this point the fat people are likely to retreat back to the television set from whence they came, which is unfortunate because brisk walking burns up four to six times as many calories as watching television.

While conducting their study on cardiovascular function, M.L. Pollock and his associates measured the effects of walking on body composition. Prior to embarking on their walking program, the twenty-four men were checked for body weight, fat percentages, and girth measurements. In the case of the control group of eight who did not walk, those factors showed no change at the end of twenty weeks. But the walkers showed losses in body weight of up to six and a half pounds and losses in fat of up to three percent. Both abdominal and gluteal measurements decreased. These reductions came from energy expenditures that began at 241 calories per session of two and a half miles of walking. This increased to 357 calories expended near the end of the program when the men walked on the treadmill at three and a quarter miles per hour.

Another study conducted by Dr. Grant Gwinup, an expert on obesity at the University of California, points out the longer term benefits of walking versus weight. A group of women who were unable to lose weight by dieting were put on a rigorous walking program of two to three hours per day. At the end of a year's walking the women had lost an average of twenty-two pounds each and were eating more than when they began.

Dr. Gwinup explains why walking for slimming provides better visual results and how the body burns up fat: "The weight loss you get from walking is general. You lose weight from all over your body. The reason for this is that whenever you use a muscle or a group of muscles they send out hormonal signals to every fat cell in your body. These cells release fat molecules into the bloodstream, which takes them to the working muscles to be used as fuel. You don't draw only on the fat near the muscle being exercised; you draw evenly on your total reserves."

In measuring fat content of the body it is the percentage that counts. Charts that show height/ weight numbers can hide up to twenty pounds of unhealthy fat. For normal people there are accepted values of fat as a percentage of body weight. Women have more body fat (and in different places) than men so the values are different for the sexes. Reasonably fit females are allowed 20 to 25 percent body fat while males should have 15 to 20 percent. Athletes and those that pursue ultimate svelteness often have less than 10 percent body fat.

Physiologists calculate individual fat weight by densitometric analysis which involves weighing a person first in water, then out of it. Fat weight and the percentage of weight in fat are then arrived at from these two figures. Walkers without access to laboratories can reach a verdict using a handy rule of thumb suggested by Dr. Donald Norfolk in *The Habits of Health*. Grasp a fold of skin at a point midway between the groin and navel and on the

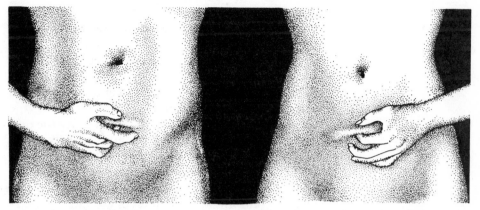

center line of the body. Women are too fat if the fold of the skin is thicker than their thumb. For men the fold should be no thicker than their little finger.

Walking versus fat

The following chart is from the book *Energy, Work and Leisure* by the Scottish team of R. Passmore and J. Durning, published in 1967. It demonstrates how walking burns up fat/calories by showing the relationship between energy expenditure (in kilocalories per minute) and the speed of walking (in miles per hour) and gross body weight (in pounds).

Calories burned per minute, related to walking speed and body weight

Speed (mph)	Body Weight (Pounds)						
	80	100	120	140	160	180	200
2.0	1.9	2.2	2.6	2.9	3.2	3.5	3.8
2.5	2.3	2.7	3.1	3.5	3.8	4.2	4.5
3.0	2.7	3.1	3.6	4.0	4.4	4.8	5.3
3.5	3.1	3.6	4.2	4.6	5.0	5.4	6.1
4.0	3.5	4.1	4.7	5.2	5.8	6.4	7.0

The chart gives caloric expense figures for walking on level ground. As in walking for aerobic capacity, intensities increase when walking on inclines, on rough ground, and on soft surfaces.

To see how walking away from fat is accomplished we can create a mythical 140 pound walker and apply their situation to the chart. On average it takes about 15 calories per pound of body weight just for normal daily maintenance. Therefore our 140 pound person can consume 2100 calories per day without experiencing any weight gain. But any caloric consumption over and above that figure will be reflected in the figure of our walker unless the extra calories are burned off in extra activity.

Suppose the 140 pounder overindulges to the tune of 200 calories per day which must be walked off. The chart shows that a person of this weight burns up 5.2 calories per minute while walking at a speed of 4 miles per hour. By dividing 5.2 into 200 calories we arrive at the number of minutes of walking necessary for the 140 pound person to keep the scales at bay. In this case 39 minutes of walking at 4 miles per hour will burn up the 200 calories. Most reasonably fit people can keep up a pace of 4 miles per hour for this period of time but those 200 calories can be used up just as easily at lesser speeds, though it will take longer. Should the 140 pound walker prefer a more leisurely pace of 3 miles per hour, the chart shows that 4 calories will be used per minute of walking. Using the same formula as before, the necessary walking time works out to 50 minutes (200 calories divided by 4).

Our 140 pound person could lose 200 calories in ways other than walking. Running for 17 minutes at 5.7 miles per hour, cycling for 36 minutes at 5.5 miles per hour, or swimming for 91 minutes at 2.2 miles per hour would achieve the same results. Playing tennis for 28 minutes, dancing for 38 minutes, or golfing for 40 minutes would also use up 200 calories.

When sleeping the 140 pound walker would probably snooze off 70 calories in one hour. One hour's exercising the jaw muscles in eating or conversation would consume about 110 calories. Playing a violin or piano would likely use up 140 calories, as would driving a car for an hour. Were the car to break down and the driver attempt to repair it, the effort would burn about 250 calories per hour. Gardening for one hour is worth about 280 calories, while a pick and shovel session for the same period of time would get rid of 400 calories.

Winter walkers can use snowshoes or cross country skis to continue the good work of walking. Skating, too, is akin to walking and all these sports leave calories out in the cold. A recent survey conducted by the Fitness Institute in Canada rated cross country skiing, squash, jogging, cycling, tennis, swimming, downhill skiing, and golf. These sports were analyzed according to cardio-respiratory fitness, muscular strength, flexibility, balance, agility/mobility, and tension release. The activities finished in the order listed, with walking on snow via skis coming out on top. Cross country skiing burns up from 600 to over 1000 calories per hour.

Continuous effort which uses up 350 calories or more per hour calls for unusual hardiness. In the case of long distance running and in sprinting, approximately 900 and 1400 calories are expended in an hour. Physics teaches us that to move a given weight requires as much energy whether it is moved fast or slowly. Six miles of hard running burns up only 20 percent more calories than walking for the same distance. The prolonged, rhythmic, moderate endurance activity that is walking enables calories to be consumed at a rate tolerable to almost any body.

If through lack of walking and calorie overloading the 140 pound person should develop into a 160 pound person or more, it is dangerous to attempt to walk off the extra weight too quickly. Slow but sure wins the race. A safe bet would be a walking program that consumes about 100 to 200 calories per day and brings about a weight loss of between one and two pounds per month. If the 160 pound person who should really weigh 140 pounds walks at a pace of 2.5 miles per hour, the chart shows that they will burn up 3.8 calories per minute. Therefore (200 calories divided by 3.8) they will need to walk for 53 minutes a day.

Winter walking leaves calories out in the cold.

How walking wins the race

The experts say that any activity using major muscle groups, that can be maintained continuously, and that is aerobic and rhythmic in nature qualifies as a way of achieving and maintaining fitness. Many of these activities will produce results faster than walking. But the tortoise and the hare parable prevails, as do several factors which help walking win the race.

In their study, "Effects of walking on body composition and cardiovascular function of middle-aged men", Pollock and his associates discussed walking as a training regimen: "The drop-out rate for men in this project was less than 25 percent, which was low in contrast to the 30 to 40 percent rate found in our previous (non-walking) investigations. This was thought to be partially a result of group cohesiveness developed while walking, decreased orthopedic problems of the leg and knee, and a more tolerable working rate."

Walking requires neither special equipment nor excessive exertion.

Walking is sociable. Long distance runners are lonely and often speechless as they engage in a silent struggle with pain. Runners and joggers tend to pursue their activities with stiff-jawed determination and flaring nostrils that preclude gregariousness. Swimmers need their mouths for breathing and their eyes get full of water. Tennis players are often too angry to speak and should they desire to communicate they must do so in a loud voice. Golfers' heads are usually filled with numbers of strokes and/or anguish. Because it takes place at such a comfortable, relaxed and manageable pace, walking is an inherently social exercise for those who are so inclined. Its lack of competition spawns congeniality and, as Oliver Wendell Holmes observed, walking frees the mind so that whatever it contains is able to come forth more easily. "In walking the will and the muscles are so accustomed to working together and perform their task with so little expenditure of force that the intellect is left comparatively free."

Walking is painless. Runners and joggers are beset with orthopedic problems referred to by Pollock et al. Studies indicate that those beginning to run or jog develop foot and knee injuries when the intensity of their training is increased above thirty minute sessions, three days a week. This means that they must risk injury to barely fulfill the minimum exercise requirements for overall fitness benefits. Walkers rarely experience anything worse than blisters, which can easily be prevented. Improper footwear and bad posture may cause temporary difficulties in sedentary people, but these can usually be eliminated. Pain is not a necessary concomitant of fitness. An exercise does not have to be hurting to be working. The sport of walking is injury and anxiety free and a walking person need never be interrupted for injury recovery time.

Walking feels good. "The more tolerable working rate" referred to in the Pollock study is an attribute unique to walking. At the conclusion of a jaunt, walkers need not stagger across a finish line in agony and collapse in an exhausted heap. A brisk walk is invigorating without being debilitating. More strenuous activities often cause intense physical and mental stress but walking feels good all the way.

Walking is cheap. Cycling, skiing, racquet sports, golf, and most other types of recreation require money to be spent before benefits can be reaped. Even running, which began as an inexpensive activity, has now become burdened by costly paraphernalia.

Walking is accessible to all. There are no mental, physical, sexual, skill, or age barriers or requirements. Even the ailing and the infirm can participate.

Few other exercises provide the opportunity for prolonged glee.

Walking needs no special equipment outside of a good pair of shoes and no court, grounds, track, green, pool, gear, sticks, balls, pads, uniforms, gadgets, timetables, schedules, whistles, or rules.

All walkers are winners. A walker does not have to come in first to succeed. The rewards come to every walker almost immediately, yet walkers do not need any specific athletic skills that must be honed and sharpened for years to be a champion.

Walking is fun. It is seldom possible to seriously engage in any other form of exercise without experiencing something less than good humor. It is possible to walk for miles with glee, and for a lifetime with pleasure.

CHAPTER FIVE

"My feet, they haul me Round the
House,
They Hoist me up the stairs;
I only have to steer them, and
They Ride me Everywheres."
Gelett Burgess

5

Meet Your Feet

The foot as a phenomenon, its characteristics, quirks and behavior, and a random peek at feet in general.

Consider the plight of the six billion or so downtrodden feet of this world. In a lifetime, constantly called upon to perform with amazing strength and endurance, they are miserably abused and neglected. Perhaps because our feet are the parts of the body furthest away from the brain, we tend to take them for granted. Or it may simply be due to the fact that most of the time they are hidden inside shoes and are sorely neglected. Whatever the reasons, no one can afford to ignore them. The mysteries of feet must be uncovered and their efforts on our behalf appreciated if we are to walk well.

From the moment an average child takes its first steps at 13.7 months the feet are in for a rough ride. It is all work and no play until they arrive at an average journey's end of seventy years. By that time a typical pair of feet will have logged approximately 70,000 miles, the equivalent of twenty-eight coast to coast crossings of the North American continent, or about three trips around the world. Give or take a few miles that works out to about 2.75 miles every day — not nearly enough to keep fit but a long haul from the point of view of the working feet carrying the often thoughtless person to whom they are attached.

Each mile an average person walks requires 2640 steps. If that person happens to weigh 150 pounds, the feet bear the brunt of 396,000 pounds of person per mile. Transferring those pounds to tons and multiplying them by 2.75 miles per day is little comfort for our abused feet; neither is the fact that a lot of people weigh more than 150 pounds. In terms of tons, however, transporting a 150 pound cargo subjects a pair of feet to a work load of 545 tons every day.

Small wonder that the feet often don't take this kind of punishment without complaining. Podiatrists estimate that eighty percent of all feet are not well. Sick feet stand alongside the common cold and headaches as the most common of man's malaises. America's number one skin disease is athlete's foot. And feet seem to be accident prone; most accidents occur in the home and twenty-five percent of these involve the feet. Industry forfeits enormous sums of money through lost man hours caused by injured or fatigued feet. In fact, suffering feet are an industry in themselves. Americans pay out about one billion dollars annually for treatment by foot specialists and for powders, salves, acids, arch supports, and other drugstore remedies.

Indeed, feet deserve our sympathy. But more than that, they need our understanding and care if they are to serve us faithfully in their appointed task of walking and a better grasp of the physiology of feet may raise our level of foot-consciousness.

Inside feet

Considering the fact that each foot was originally designed to carry only one quarter of our body weight, they bear up amazingly well. Our hands — feet that gave up walking long ago — have been left far behind as a means of locomotion. A normal, healthy set of feet can cover many miles without tiring but a pair of hands would be hard pressed to travel more than a yard or two. Although they do not have the same prehensile capabilities as hands, when called upon feet can summon up a fair imitation of a hand. This is demonstrated by people who have learned to paint and perform other activities normally done by hand. Ballet dancers, too, show that it is possible to develop great neuromuscular control of the feet. Generally speaking, however, the function of feet is to support

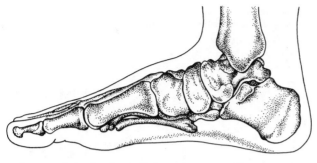

One quarter of all the bones in the body are located in the feet.

and propel the body and they are magnificently well-engineered to do that.

A foot is usually described as having twenty-six bones, some of them among the smallest in the body. Every foot has, in addition, two small round bones that lie hidden at the bottom of the foot behind the big toe. Because these two sesamoid bones, floating independently in tendons, play no part in walking, they are often overlooked. (The only time they count is when a foot is x-rayed.) The recognized twenty-six bones join up with each other to allow movement. Seven of them make up the *tarsus*, located immediately below the ankle. Then come the five bones of the *metatarsus;* the remaining fourteen are in the toes. Strangely enough the big toe has only two bones while the others each have three. In fact, despite its name, it is not always the biggest. Thirty-one percent of big toes are actually exceeded in length by either of the two digits alongside them — the great toe (immediately next to the big one) and the second toe. The third toe lies in relative obscurity next to the little toe.

The arrangement of bones in the foot forms two arches. The first one, found in the area usually called the ball of the foot, is the metatarsal arch. The longitudinal arch is the concave area extending from the heel to the ball on the inner side of your foot. This is the arch that is prone to falling. Should you happen to be born with a very low or flat longitudinal arch you could be described as a "congenital flatfoot". Your flat or pronated feet derive from the Latin word *pronus* meaning prone. They are sometimes labeled *pes planus* (from *pedes* — feet and *planus* — flat, in Latin). Whatever label

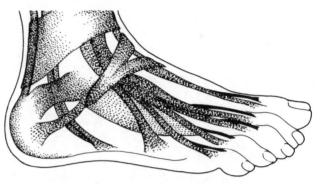

Footpower is generated by many marvelous muscles.

you wish to apply to them, your flat feet may not look particularly graceful but they will stand you in good stead in the event of a forced march. Contrary to the state of affairs during World War I when those with flat feet were rejected as unsuitable for duty, congenital flatfooters were welcomed with open arms in World War II. Between the two conflicts it was discovered that flat feet were the least likely to suffer under the stress of long marches.

Ligaments, fifty-six of them, are the tough bands of flexible fibrous tissue that bind the bones together at the joints. The joints in the feet, all of them movable, are activated by thirty-eight muscles controlling both the extent and direction of movement. One of the most prominent of these is the *extensor brevis digitorum* on the top of the foot, just in front of the ankle toward the outer side. *Extensor brevis* and the other muscles are connected to the bones by tendons.

Achilles and heels

The most notorious tendon, named after the late Greek hero Achilles, can be a sore point. When the muscles at the back of the leg contract in a walking step they tug on the *tendo-Achilles*, raising the heel off the ground. The Achilles tendon often objects and well it might. The force exerted on it at that moment is equal to twice the body weight of the walker. Sometimes that force actually pulls the heel out of position, causing the foot to roll over on its side, which can lead to pronation.

The Greeks and Romans admired the Achilles heel for its beauty and exposed it in their leather

54

sandals. Its importance in walking is gruesomely illustrated by the fact that Greek slaves, or *cretati*, had their Achilles tendons slashed to keep them from running away. (*Cretati*, meaning chalked people, were identified by their chalked soles when sold in the slave market.) As a symbol of vulnerability, the tendon is aptly named.

Although a hero of the Trojan war, Achilles himself had a certain notoriety, tending to be temperamental and quarrelsome. Included in the attentions lavished upon him by his doting mother, Thesis, was an almost, but not quite total immersion in the River Styx. It was her belief that this would make her special baby immortal. To accomplish this she dunked her squirming son in the magical waters, grasping him by the heel so as not to lose him. Unfortunately for Achilles and for those that followed, Thesis failed to realize that the part of his body in her hand remained quite mortal. And so he went off to war with a vulnerable heel.

During the battle with the Trojans Achilles had a disagreement with his commander, Agamemnon, and in a fit of pique retired to his tent, refusing to fight. He remained there until his close friend Patroclus was killed by the Trojan warrior, Hector. This served to galvanize Achilles into action. He slew Hector and dragged his body by the heels three times around the walls of Troy. To avenge the death of Hector, Paris shot a poisoned arrow into the

Achilles' heel helped cause the sack of Troy.

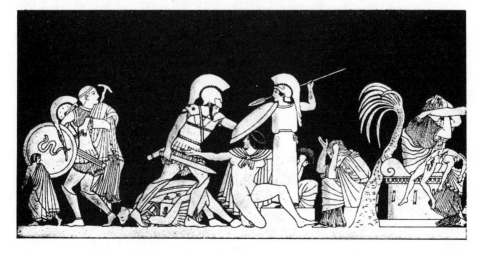

55

mortal heel of Achilles, dropping him in his tracks. Although failing to prevent the sacking of Troy, it did make a hero of Achilles and did provide a name for that tendon in the back of your foot.

No doubt an autopsy on Achilles would have revealed that death was caused by the poison from the arrow entering the bloodstream. As is the case in the rest of the body, blood is the source of nourishment for the muscles and bones of the feet. The fact that he died rather quickly indicates that Achilles had good circulation, often a rare condition today. Because the feet are furthest away from the heart they are usually the first area to reveal circulatory problems.

Footpulse

"The heart is in accord with the pulse." Since feet are the heart of the matter in walking, these words from Huang Ti, the Yellow Emperor of China, have special significance. Most people might check their pulse on their wrists; walkers can do it on their feet in two places where the arteries are most prominent. The *dorsalis pedis* is on the top of the foot in a line between the big toe and the toe next to it. The *posterior tibial* pulse can be located behind the bone on the inner side of the ankle. The fact that Huang Ti lived from 2697 to 2597 B.C. suggests that his heart, pulse, and feet must have been in perfect accord.

It has not been disclosed whether Huang Ti took his pulse in his feet but chances are its rate was somewhere between 60 and 75 beats a minute, the average rate. As Plutarch said, sometime between 46 and 120 A.D.: "Each person ought neither to be unacquainted with the peculiarities of his own pulse, for there are many individual diversities." To allow for those fluctuations, a count between 50 and 100 is considered to be a normal resting rate.

After a spate of walking your feet will register from 100 to 140, as shown in the last chapter, depending on your speed and physical condition. Another way of making the blood flow faster into your feet is to place them in close proximity to another pair of desirable feet. Your pulse will accelerate because it is affected by emotion as well as activity.

56

The rest of the plumbing system of the feet is made up of veins and capillaries. The latter are the tiny vessels which connect the veins with the arteries. Most feet have a bluish arc on the top of the foot beginning just behind the toes and continuing up towards the ankle. These are the veins responsible for carrying the used blood back to the heart from the feet. Like the arteries, there is nothing like a brisk walk to help the veins do their duty. The massaging action of the contracting and relaxing muscles in a walking foot encourages the pipeline of blood vessels to circulate their precious cargo.

The skin of the foot encloses all vital parts in a neat package, decorated and embellished with toenails. On the top of the foot this wrapping of skin is as thin as an eyelid, while at the sole and heel it can measure up to one and a half inches, which is thicker than anywhere else on your body. This provides shock absorbing benefits as well as being a handy source of extra skin should you ever have the misfortune to require a graft.

So there it stands — the basic foot. To bring it to life, to animate it, to make it walk, we require nerves which play an important role in the life support system of your feet. They carry impulses from the brain that make feet get up and go by stimulating the muscles, then relay information back to the brain with regular reports as to where those feet are going. They also give feeling to your feet. Despite the intricate network of nerves and nervous impulses, however, feet suffer from their isolation. Compared to the hands, for instance, the area of the brain devoted to the feet is very small.

Footsteps

In the normal walking stride each foot spends approximately sixty percent of its time on the ground. The remaining forty percent finds it swinging through the air to take up a position ahead of the supporting foot. During the period of ground contact the foot does all the work. Every time your heel lifts off the ground it forces the toes to carry one half of your body weight. The toes respond when they take off, leaving the heel with a vertical load that actually exceeds body weight by twenty-five percent.

This does not mean that the heel and toe are adversaries. On the contrary, they work hand in hand with each other as the foot is designed to distribute the body load evenly over all its parts. The interconnected muscles and bones floating around inside their sack of skin have the looseness and adaptability of a bean bag so that they can conform to even or uneven surfaces. When the heel touches the ground, the weight is carried along the outer border of the foot to the ball, then across the ball to the big toe. Rough surfaces make it easier for the bean bag principle to work.

Feet came in for a hard time of it with encroaching civilization. Fragile bones and soft tissues were much more at home on soil and jungle grass than taking a beating on unyielding concrete, asphalt, and hard floors. Their original environment allowed the feet to develop all the muscles in an unrestricted manner and helped distribute the work of walking evenly throughout the feet.

However, as well as being flexible, feet are made of strong stuff. Despite evolution, they have adapted to the rigors of the modern world, and have not changed to a great degree since man first stood upright. At birth, ninety-eight percent of all feet are considered to be normal. But normal as applied to feet has a variety of interpretations.

Footwatching

The truth of the matter is that no two feet are exactly the same; one of them is always larger than the other. Some people might consider this to be a defect, whereas seekers of beauty and truth know that all great works of art are not precision made. Deviances from the norm and tiny imperfections add up to a greater whole, giving strength of character and depth of meaning. Every pair of feet is asymmetrical to say the least, and beautiful and functional because of it. A quick glance at the soles of a new pair of shoes should point out the differences between each foot when you walk.

An old English rhyme which equates the wear on soles with the quality of life suggests that you could read your fortune from your feet.

Tip at the toe, live to see woe;
Wear at the side, live to be a bride;
Wear at the ball, live to spend all;
Wear at the heel, live to save a deal.

In ancient Greece, Aristophanes said: "It is right that each man should measure himself by his feet." In Rome, Pliny the Elder later played with this profundity and made the following discovery: "It has been observed that the height of a man from the sole of the foot to the crown of the head is equal to the distance between the tips of the middle fingers of the two hands when extended in a straight line."

Your sole searching will also indicate whether or not your foot is distributing your weight properly when walking. Ideally, signs of wear should cover the back of the heel of the shoe and be spread evenly over the whole of the sole, beginning in front of the arch and extending to the toe, but excluding the inner rim. If you have a worn inner rim you might be flatfooted. Don't be alarmed if your shoe leather does not match. Credit it to a unique pair of feet.

Footprint folklore

The Lone Ranger's faithful companion, Tonto, was able to tell a great deal about an outlaw by the footprints he left behind. Sherlock Holmes had similar capabilities and could establish personality traits as well as physical characteristics from a criminal's footprint.

Many cultures in the past and even today place great stock in the connection between the person and their footprints. The Seneca Indian tribe of North America felt that animals shared this phenomenon so that a bear knew when a hunter was looking at his track and would begin to take suitable evasive action. Certain Australian aborigines believe that magic can be worked on a person by dealing with the mark of their foot left in the earth, in ashes, or in sand. Some of them endeavor to harm their enemies by putting sharp stones or glass in their footprints. In Burma and India sores on the feet are often attributed to interference with one's footprints by an enemy or a witch. For this same reason some

Africans take care to obliterate their tracks. Insects which scurry back and forth to blot out the tracks of hunters and warriors are revered by certain tribes.

In old Bohemia it was thought possible to lame a man by scooping up the earth containing his footprint and putting it in a kettle along with a nail, a needle, and some broken glass. The mixture was then boiled until the kettle cracked, whereupon it was believed that the unfortunate victim of this witchcraft would be lame for the rest of their life. Lithuanians felt that if the dust of a person's footprint were sprinkled in a graveyard, they would sicken and die. To achieve the same results Estonians could measure the length of the track with a stick and bury that length.

Footprints as love charms were used by some of the early people in the southern United States. The person of one's desire could be captured if the earth or sand of their footprint was tied up in a red flannel bag and carried on one's person. To ensure a faithful husband, a Zulu woman kept the soil of the man's footprint near her bed.

Folktales tell of magic footprints which would transform whoever stepped in them into a variety of beasts and demons, depending on who left the prints. In one Icelandic saga, footprints are used as a symbol of the fate of heroes. If the print was filled with earth, the hero was sick; if with water, he was drowned; if it filled with blood, he was killed in battle. Local legends around the world identify marks on rocks and mountains as the footprints of gods, demons, and other supernatural beings. Variations on the Abominable Snowman theme are found in almost every society.

Naked feet

Down through the ages the naked foot has had trouble gaining acceptance. Plutarch, a Greek contemporary of Pliny, felt that bare feet were a sign of a slave's degradation. Though they were quite free with their noses, Eskimos regarded the showing of feet as extremely immodest. In Victorian times, when the word "leg" was considered to be an obscenity in the English language, naked feet were

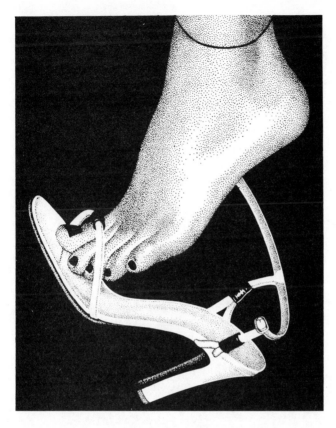

*An indication of the
breakdown of society
— or a thing of
beauty?*

taboo. Even today certain business establishments
refuse to serve a barefooted customer. Unshod feet
are often interpreted as a sign of undisciplined
behavior, perhaps even perversity, and at the very
least another indication of the breakdown of society.

This only serves to make bare feet symbols of
freedom. One of the first things the hippie genera-
tion shed, along with other conventions, were shoes.
"Barefoot Vacations" are considered to be the
ultimate in get-away-from-it-all holidays. Inside
quite a few shoes there are bare feet struggling to get
out. Many otherwise well balanced people nurse a
secret desire to free their feet from their bonds and
walk away from all their trials and tribulations.

John Burroughs, (1837-1921), the U.S. naturalist
who walked (often in the company of Walt
Whitman) and wrote about walking, paid tribute to
naked feet in his *Exhilarations of the Road:*

61

"Occasionally on the sidewalk, amid the dapper, swiftly-moving, high-heeled boots and gaiters, I catch a glimpse of the naked human foot. Nimbly it scuffs along, the toes spread, the sides flatten, the heel protrudes; it grasps the curbing, or bends to the form of the uneven surfaces — a thing sensuous and alive, that seems to take cognisance of whatever it touches or passes. How primitive and uncivil it looks in such company — a real barbarian in the parlour. We are so unused to the human anatomy, to simple, unadorned nature, that it looks a little repulsive; but it is beautiful for all that. Though it be a black foot and unwashed foot, it shall be exalted. It is a thing of life amid leather, a free spirit amid cramped, a wild bird amid caged, an athlete amid consumptives. It is the symbol of my order, the Order of Walkers. That unhampered, vitally playing piece of anatomy is the type of pedestrian, man returned to first principles, in direct contact and intercourse with the earth and the elements, his faculties unsheathed, his mind plastic, his body toughened, his heart light, his soul dilated: while those cramped and distorted members in the calf and kid are the unfortunate wretches doomed to carriages and cushions."

Sensuous feet

Our feet are great pleasure centers. The liberating effect of releasing fretting feet from the imprisonment of confining clodhoppers is a positive joy. It really is "a treat to beat your feet on the Mississippi mud" and there are few sensual thrills the equal of walking barefoot over a carpet of soft, green grass or along a stretch of sun-drenched and deserted sandy beach. Cooling your heels in a sparkling mountain stream at the end of a hike is one of walking's great rewards. The affinity of feet with water may be a throwback to our aquatic ancestry. The Hardy Theory of Aquatic Man says that water played a prime part in our past. One survey of the feet of a thousand schoolchildren revealed that nine percent of the boys and more than six and a half percent of the girls had webbing between the second and third toes.

Feet are among the prime organs of sensuality.

Soles come close to armpits as being the most ticklish area of the body. Some people find them erotic and a strong case might be made for their inclusion with those parts of the body qualifying as erogenous zones. Liberated lovers have long taken pleasure in playing "footsie", a practice that Johann Wolfgang von Goethe may have indulged in. During his tenure as ‚he greatest poet, scientist, statesman, and devotee of dainty feet in the duchy of Weimar in Germany, he pronounced: "A pretty foot is a great gift of nature."

But when it comes to kissing, feet have traditionally been held in low esteem. "Kiss my foot" or "Bite my foot" are less than complimentary terms. In his book, *Intimate Behaviour,* Desmond Morris points out that when we choose a site to bestow a kiss on someone as a show of respect, we tend to work from the top down. We choose "the cheek, for friendly equality; the hand, for deep respect; the knee for humble submission and the foot, for grovelling servility." In the case of fawning and complete abasement we "bite the dust" or become a crawling "boot-licker".

Playing "footsie" is an ancient game.

Perspiration may be one of the reasons why feet are shunned in sex. Certainly some feet smell less than sweet. Normal body odors are attractive to the opposite sex and since olden times have been considered to be an aphrodisiac. Oriental potentates would have the beauties of their harem work up a sweat and make their choice by sniffing out the most attractive scent from a pile of the ladies' clothes and shoes.

Today deodorants and foot powders foil the scent. Sniffing shoes and smelling feet are now left mainly to dogs who excel at it. We leak about a pint of perspiration each day, ninety-nine and a half percent of it water and only a tiny portion of it through the soles of our feet. Each footstep carries 250 billion molecules of butyric acid, an aromatic substance which a canine can detect several days after a person has walked by.

Some aspects of the behavior of feet might indicate that their feelings run deeper than they are generally given credit for. They display a surprising variety of emotions. Temper tantrums are often accompanied by an irately stamping foot. A foot that is bored stiff tends to tap with impatience, as does an exasperated foot. Many feet celebrate the joy of music by tapping in time with a delightful ditty.

These goings-on lend credence to the idea of "foot reflexology", a theory which suggests that certain charted areas of the foot have energy or nerve connections with some specific part of the body. By applying pressure to the foot it is possible to have a therapeutic effect elsewhere. Similarly, in acupuncture pins are stuck into the sole of the foot to treat problems far away from the feet, including toothache, backache, and abdominal pain.

Sore feet

It is a medical fact that the first indication of systemic disease often comes to light in the feet. Ulcers, brittle nails, dry skin, and a tingling or numbness in the feet can be caused by diabetes. Tumors, arthritis, swelling, and circulation disorders that show up in the feet usually herald trouble elsewhere in the body. Acquired flat feet, as opposed to the congenital kind, are often caused by ligament defects further up the line in the leg.

In the 1930s sufferers from arthritis, neuritis, sciatica, synovitis, and so forth placed their feet in the hands of Dr. M.W. Locke who based his entire practice on his belief that: "Nobody can feel well if his feet are sick." One lady with an arthritic shoulder questioned his technique. When she arrived at his office in Williamsburg in Ontario, Canada, Dr. Locke didn't bother to look at her shoulder, but treated her arches instead. "But doctor! It isn't my foot that hurts. It's my shoulder."

"I know," he replied, "but if you step on a dog's tail, which end of him yelps?"

CHAPTER SIX

"Her pretty feet, like snails, did
creep
A little out, and then,
As if they played at bo-peep,
Did soon draw in again."
Robert Herrick

6

Footcare

Basic foot hygiene, some complaints and their cures, treats for feet, and some paces to put them through.

"I treat my feet like premature twins," says John Hillaby, the celebrated British pedestrian. For a walker, footcare should be as basic as hair brushing and teeth cleaning. But since feet are more complicated and sensitive than hair and teeth, their proper care and grooming requires more than a once-over-lightly session.

Foot hygiene

Bathe your feet just after waking up and before going to bed at night with a mild soap and water at a temperature of 85° to 90°F. Soap well between the toes for it is here that the organisms of infection linger. Remove all traces of dead skin, stocking lint, dust, and grime. Rinse the feet thoroughly, then dry them even more thoroughly, especially between the toes because fungi and bacteria thrive in dampness, as does foot odor. Aid the drying process with commercially available sprays, talcums, or powders.

All ministrations should be performed with non-scratching, non-nicking tools. Toenails are best manicured immediately after the washing process which serves to soften them. The ground rules of trimming are designed to prevent ingrown toenails. Cut them straight across with a sharp, straight-edged nail clipper or equally endowed scissors. Don't cut the nails in the oval shape of your toe so that the top edge of the nail curves down into the

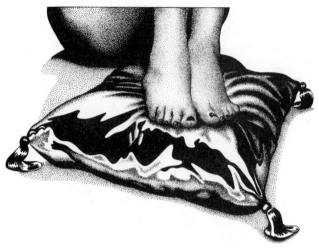

Well treated feet look and walk better.

skin at the sides. Always leave the sides parallel to the skin. To cut to the quick is to scream with pain. Do not trim any deeper than the tip of the toe. This length of nail acts as a shock absorber against the shoe, protecting the toe from pressure and friction. Smooth any rough edges with a file or emery board. Cuticle, that bit of useless epidermis or superficial skin at the base of the nails, should be kept at bay. Gently push it back with a cotton swab.

Change your socks frequently and wash them after every wearing. Have at least two pairs of walking shoes and wear them on alternate days. Put the pair not in use out to air. Take off the laces and open the throats so that they can dry out completely. Dusting powders help them dry and snuff out odors. Shoes are like toothbrushes. Never use anyone else's.

Foot complaints

Inspect your feet regularly. Usually you will know quickly enough if there is trouble afoot but a close inspection can help nip simple problems in the bud. If the following home remedies fail or if your foot inspection should turn up anything more serious, take your feet to a specialist as fast as they will go.

Corns and calluses, blisters gone bad, are caused by poor posture, foot imbalance, enlarged and irritated joints, or ill-fitting shoes. As a defense mechanism the foot builds up layers of skin to help relieve the pressure against the shoe. This extra skin hardens into calluses, then full-fledged corns which are deeper and cover a wider area. Their pressure on the underlying layers of skin is what causes the pain. Soaking your feet in warm water will provide temporary relief. Rub lanolin into the offending areas and apply thin pads of cotton wool to ease the pressure inside your shoe. Because of the danger of infection it is best not to cut or trim them yourself but you can rub them with special lava stones which are available for the purpose.

Ingrown nails are the result of improper trimming, shoes that are too short or too narrow, or foot imbalance, any of which will cause the nail to press and cut into the flesh as it grows. If the condition has not gone too far, you can alleviate the pressure by first cleaning carefully beneath the nail. Next, gently insert a wisp of cotton wool under the ingrown corner. To accomplish this delicate operation use a blunt toothpick or cotton swab.

Athlete's foot is a form of ringworm that will make your feet distinctly non-athletic. Should you find the cracks, raw and red skin, blisters, or itching of this nasty condition between your toes, it means that a fungus or mold is growing there. Scrubbing and soaking the feet for about ten minutes in warm, soapy water will help get rid of it. Follow this with a reputable fungus-killing preparation.

Excessively wet or dry feet can be treated at home. Perspiring feet can be helped by sprays or powders and by buying socks made of wool (which absorbs perspiration) or cotton. Feet with dry skin can be doctored with lanolin, baby oil, or foot cream.

Cold feet, one of the most common of foot complaints, are caused by tight footwear or poor circulation. The quickest relief, other than plenty of walking, is a hot-water soak.

Your regular surveys should also seek out the signs of more serious foot ailments. Heaven forbid that you should find them, but the sad statistics show that all too many feet are susceptible to a plague of problems, some of which are: Dermatitis (skin inflammations); Plantar Wart (on the soles); Bunions (swollen big toe joints); Diabetes Mellitus (indicated by numbness); Arthritis (inflammation in the joints); Foot Strain (tired and aching feet); Morton's Toe (tumors between the bones). All of these, as well as foot deformities and the more prevalent fallen arches and Achilles heel problems, can usually be successfully treated by foot specialists.

Treats for your feet

Happy feet have slim people on top. One of the first favors you can do for your feet is to lighten their load by losing weight. Obesity weakens foot structure and contributes to fallen arches. Heavy people and their feet tend to perspire more than slender types, encouraging foot infections and odors. Chubby toes are more prone to ingrown toenails. The best cure for fat feet is, of course, a steady diet of walking.

Whether you are fat or thin, take the load off your feet frequently. Putting your feet up whenever possible helps improve your circulation and gives them a new perspective. Even when standing for long periods of time, you can rest your feet somewhat by alternately standing on the inside and outside of your feet. Another way of resting while standing involves the ballet stance of pointing one foot straight ahead and placing the other beside it at a forty-five degree angle, with the rear foot's heel to the forward foot's sole.

Give your feet a breather during the day by taking them out of your shoes. This gives the air a chance to get at your feet and shoes. It also helps you and your feet to relax. The possibility that this action may have the reverse effect on your colleagues at work can be overcome by doing it under your desk.

Go barefoot at the slightest provocation. Do it on sand, grass, carpeting, or other resilient surfaces. Shoes insulate your feet from these pleasures. Sunbathe your bare feet but take care to avoid sunburn which can happen quickly on feet with sensitive skin. Tired feet respond well to a good soaking in warm water. It should not be too hot, since tender feet are only made more so by heat.

A post-walking massage is a rewarding experience for feet. You can do it yourself if a foot masseur/

masseuse is not available. Concentrate your massage on those spots that are sore or tender using brief firm pressure from your fingers. The key to a successful massage is to alternate each deep movement with a softer one. Make rhythmical kneading movements of pressure, working from the ankle to the toes, then back again. Ten minutes of this per foot can do wonders to restore circulation.

Foot exercises

Walking is the best all-round conditioner for feet. But even that activity leaves some of the foot out of the action and tends to involve the repetition of the same movements. In addition, shoes — no matter how good they are — restrict and limit the full use of muscles and range of movements of which the feet are capable. Thus, well-rounded feet need special exercising.

Perform these exercises in your bare feet. Although they can be done anywhere at any time, try to develop them into a regular routine, perhaps before or after your foot ablutions. For full benefit do the exercises at least three times a week. As well, they can be a pleasant and helpful interlude in the middle of a long walk.

These first exercises give your feet an extra workout while walking. Do each movement for about thirty seconds.

1. Walk normally, but at the end of each step — just as the ball of the foot strikes the floor — push up high on to your tiptoes before starting the next step.

2. Walk on your heels, holding your toes high.

3. Walk on the inside portion of each foot.

4. Walk on the outside edge of each foot.

The next set of exercises is performed while standing. Repeat each movement several times.

1. Rise up on the tips of your toes and hold this position for a moment. Then lower your heels as slowly as possible. Do this first with your feet pointing straight ahead, then pointing inward, and finally pointing outward.

2. Keeping the heel and ball of each foot on the ground, raise your arches as high as you can. Hold it for a moment, then relax your arch slowly.

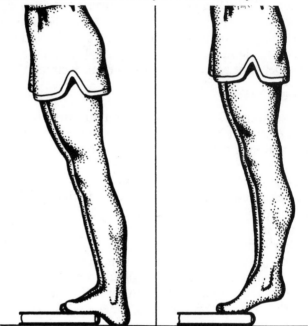

3. Place the balls of your feet on a book or some similar object about two inches thick. With your heels firmly against the floor, lean forward as far as you can without lifting your heels. Then rise up on your toes bringing your heels off the floor.

The following sequence of movements is performed while you sit with your feet on the floor with your knees up. Each of the ten movements should be held for a count of five seconds with a two second relaxing period between each one.

1. Raise your toes as high as you can while keeping the heel and ball of each foot on the floor.

2. Spread your toes as wide apart as possible and hold them that way.

3. Squeeze them together as hard as you can.

4. Press your toes firmly against the floor.

5. Extend your toes forward to their full length.

6. Raise your arches as high as possible while keeping your heels and toes on the floor.

7. With your heels resting on the floor raise the rest of each foot as high as you can, pointing your toes toward the ceiling.

8. Roll your upper feet inward so that their outside edges are as high as possible.

9. Roll your feet outward so that the arches face upward.

10. Lift both feet off the floor and clap the soles together vigorously.

Perform this final sequence of movements while sitting on the floor with your legs straight out in front of you and slightly apart. For support put your arms out behind you, palms flat on the floor.

1. With your heels against the floor, point your toes as far forward as you can — reach them towards the opposite wall. Now describe a slow circle with your toes in a clockwise direction. Make five slow circles and do five more in a counter-clockwise direction.

2. Grip a pencil with your toes. Hold the pencil for five seconds, then drop it and extend your toes forward to their full length for another five seconds. Repeat the pencil performance several times with each foot.

Feet that are given proper care and a regular routine of walking supplemented by these exercises will perform their appointed task wonderfully well. This will render obsolete the chorus of a street ballad popular in London a century ago:

> All over London town
> No matter who you meet,
> There's nothing now goes down,
> But, "How is your poor feet?"

CHAPTER SEVEN

"Ye tuneful cobblers! Still your
notes prolong,
Compose at once a slipper and a
song;
So shall the fair your handiwork
peruse,
Your sonnets sure shall please —
perhaps your shoes."
Byron

7

Footwear

The saga of shoes past: the fashions and foibles of fabulous footwear, the symbolism in shoes, and pointers on outfitting feet.

To get off on the right foot in walking, the all-important first step is to select the proper footwear. What you put on your feet is the very foundation of your walking life. Since walkers are by nature reflective types and because the road to enlightenment is supposed to be paved with the profits of past experience, a look at how some of our ancestors really put their foot in it will be worthwhile.

Shoes are worn for defense, decency, and decoration — honorable reasons all. Our instincts advise us to protect our feet from the elements, society insists that we cover up potentially erotic or dirty feet, and our vanity impels us to follow the prevailing fashion. Unfortunately for feet these needs conflict causing collapses, corns, calluses, and countless other conditions that put them out of commission.

The toe of suspicion points directly at fashion as the villain in the majority of foot disorders. From the foot's point of view the basic idea of a shoe is a good one. Decency notwithstanding, a well-designed shoe provides a foot with protection from its enemies and the weather, plus valuable support in walking. But in the name of style a foot is suffocated, pinched, pounded, chafed, contorted, and squashed. It wasn't always so. The first shoes were built for go rather than show.

In the beginning there was grass, palm fronds, animal hides, and wood. There was also heat, cold,

The Egyptians discovered the necessity for a right and a left sandal some 4000 years before the rest of the civilized world.

stones and other sharp objects, and many miles to be walked. Shoeless man, utilizing the newfound intelligence which had been made possible by his feet, put two and two together and came up with sandals. The first shoe, as such, was the primitive *carbatine*, a simple sandal fashioned from a strip of raw leather and held on the foot by a threaded thong.

In colder climes animal skins were wrapped around the feet and tied with strips of rawhide. These evolved into the moccasins and soft skin boots worn by Indians and Eskimos. During intense cold the Eskimo boot was filled with dried grass or moss as insulation.

Back in the cradle of civilization other types of sandals were made of plaited grass, palm fronds, or strips of wood, fastened by thongs which passed between the toes and were bound around the ankles. In Egypt these were sold in plain or decorated styles, according to the caste of the wearer, in the shoe shops that sprang up along the banks of the Nile. It was the Egyptians who discovered a need for a right and left sandal, something which did not arrive in England until 1785 and in America until the last century. The occasional set of shoes cropped up in this period, a pair was found in King Tut's tomb, but it was the Greeks who developed sandals into shoes.

After several thousand years of hindsight it is possible to speculate why Aristotle and his peripatetic school of thinkers had such brilliant inspiration. Firstly, sandals enabled their feet to breathe freely, a necessity that plastic, rubber, and other modern materials make difficult. Secondly, this simple footwear allowed Aristotle's ankles to articulate easily so that they could move him forward more efficiently. Thirdly, the thinkers walked *upon* their sandals, not inside them, which automatically eliminated many of the chafing problems that feet find in shoes. Fourthly, the flexible sandal soles gave the thinkers a better grip on the earth and their feet were better able to adapt to landscape variances. In short the peripatetic school had happy feet and thought better because of it. As Abraham Lincoln said: "When my feet hurt, I can't think."

For hunting, Greek men wore sandals with

Abraham Lincoln couldn't think when his feet hurt.

oversize straps that eventually became solid leather which protected against thorns, serpents, and the like. By 1400 B.C. the ladies of Crete were inclined to go barefoot around the house but they wore shoes and then high boots when out for a stroll.

It seems likely that some of these first attempts at boots and shoes were slightly off the track. Corns and other foot disorders are mentioned in writings of the time and Hikesios of Smyrna prepared a corn plaster in 100 B.C. Sandals served Jesus Christ and others in the Bible, but a report in II Chronicles indicates that some of them were not up to scratch: "And Asa in the thirty and ninth month of his reign was diseased in his feet, until his disease was exceeding great; yet he sought not to the Lord, but to his physicians."

The collapse of the Roman empire was paralleled by the collapse of countless arches. At first, light sandals were *de rigeur* for everyday wear in Rome but soon the *calceus* came into vogue for full dress occasions. When this style — shoes with slits at the sides and knots in front — began to appear beneath togas, it marked the beginning of an era of tough slogging for walkers. Esthetics overruled common sense in shoe design and the basic contour of the foot was forgotten. Ever since the function of the shoe has been, for the most part, secondary to its form.

The road to ruin

From the Middle Ages the cobblers' credo was to make foot covering "fitte to a great and good nicetie". To accomplish this they turned to pointed toes and high heels with ridiculous and painful results. Strangely enough pointed toes originated as a cure for an ugly set of bunions possessed by a certain Fulk Rechin, who hobbled about in the court of William II in England. The burden of his bunions caused him to become an involuntary court jester as his contemporaries poked fun and gibes at his strange manner of walking. Fulk was vain and something of a dandy so when they began referring to him as "The Cross-looking" he decided to take action.

His solution for his troubled toes was to lengthen

"The Horned One" created a monster shoe.

his shoes and taper them to a point in order to cover up his deformity. Because he was rich and labor was cheap he had dozens of pairs of his design made up in ornate patterns and colors. The idea caught on in the court and pointed shoes became the order of the day and the route to nobility. Cornadus, an aspiring noble, took "Cross-looking's" concept to greater lengths, extending his shoes even further and twisting their tips into the shape of a ram's horn, for which *he* was nicknamed "The Horned One".

Footwear that began as Fulk's folly became a nightmare for feet. Shoes shrunk at the exact place where they should widen to admit the toes and metatarsals. Streamlined insteps unduly restricted the longitudinal arch which reacted by falling, as often as not. "The Cross-looking" and "The Horned One" had created a monster shoe in which toes screamed with the pain of corns, rigidus, hammer toes, hallux valgus, hallux flexus, hallux rigidus, metatarsalagia, and more. Their owners suffered in silence.

The fops of the period reveled in the pointed look. Shoes became narrower and toes extended to six inches and beyond so that they eventually had to be held up by chains between their points and the wearers' knees. Little bells on their toes heralded the arrival of a wearer of these seven league boots. The longer the shoe, the higher the rank of the feet inside. To preserve their badge of office the aristocracy laid down decrees relating the size of shoe extensions to a person's position in life. Ordinary foot-sloggers were allowed up to six inches; respected merchants could do business in footwear with twelve inch toes; gallant knights might try to ride their spirited chargers with eighteen inch toes — if they could get into the saddle; while a baron was welcome to survey his domain on toes of two feet. There was no limit at all for princes and kings and royalty.

The Church looked askance at these preposterous footwear fashions and made several attempts to exorcise the "little devils" that perched on the tips of shoes. But to no avail. It was the privileged long-toed ones themselves who eventually ended the custom. They found that even though their subjects had shorter ones, their awkward toes were affecting efficiency. Knights were being beaten in battle and peasants were having trouble walking and working. During the reign of Edward IV (1461–1483) a shoe reform act was passed: "No knight under the rank of lord shall wear any shoes or boots having pikes or points exceeding the length of two inches, under the forfeiture of forty pence."

Henry VIII added weight to this trend when he began to wear commoners' broad boots. His carousings and assorted excesses had caused a severe bout of gout which manifested itself in his big toes. Swollen and tinted a royal purple, Henry's toes found comfort in the more generous peasant footwear. Needless to say broad shoes soon became popular with the nobility and they widened to such a degree that Henry was forced to lay down a law establishing a six inch maximum width, applicable to all but himself, of course.

While people played with their feet in the western world, the Chinese were occupied binding the feet of females. Foot squashing persists to this day in many shoe styles but the reasons why the custom began are obscure. One theory has it that an envious Chinese empress, afflicted with a club-foot, issued an edict forcing all women to share her defect by having their feet bound at birth. Another belief places the blame with male chauvinists who wished to keep women indoors. Some foot behavioralists feel that it was intended as a status symbol: crushed feet made walking and work difficult, therefore a high class lady was above these menial pastimes. Others are of the opinion that foot binding was a relic of foot-fetishism and that Chinese women attempted to keep their men at bay with deformed and thus sexually unattractive feet.

In Europe too, the ladies were in the avant garde of the next development in the continuing saga of shoes. As toes receded, heels ascended. Actually the first high heels were worn by actors in Egyptian plays. Chinese and Japanese dramatists, too, put their leading characters on stilts to give them greater stature. Stilts were the forerunners of high heels. Devices called "pattens", wooden sandals with heels

Chopines became a stumbling block in medieval romances.

of an inch and a half, were developed to strap under shoes to protect against the wet. In Venice, with more than its share of dampness, they became higher and distinctly stilt-like and were christened *chopines*. Catherine de Medici was married in a pair in Paris, having brought them with her from Italy. Undoubtedly her husband, Henry II, admired how her *chopines* showed off her ankle and calf so beguilingly, but it is quite likely he had to carry his bride up the stairs to the boudoir as well as across the threshold. It became accepted practice for ladies to take off their shoes when negotiating stairs, or have a gallant male carry them. Soon men's heels were higher than women's and gallant males had enough trouble carrying themselves.

No one has analyzed why heels several inches off the ground should look better. These cumbersome curiosities made it difficult to dance as Shakespeare pointed out in Act I, Scene 5 of *Romeo and Juliet:* "Ah ha, my mistresses! Which of you will now deny to dance? She that makes dainty, she, I'll swear hath corns."

Had Shakespeare been podiatrically informed he might have added several other reasons why the lady could not dance or walk. (Dancing, after all, is just stylized walking performed to music.) When high heels push the weight of the whole body forward over the toes, it upsets the balance of weight-bearing power that the feet have spent a million years perfecting, placing undue stress on the middle of the metatarsus. As well, it shortens the leverage area of the foot which necessitates more muscular effort to walk, in turn increasing the energy cost of walking. It also shortens the Achilles tendon. Walking on an inclined plane distorts the foot, thus altering the poise of the body, which strains the spinal muscles and sometimes throws the internal organs out of position. Even when a high-heel wearer has seen the folly of her ways and wants to come back down to earth, the suffering will continue in low heels.

By the time James I tottered up to the throne in 1603, heels were ridiculously high and the whole silly spectacle of shoes was enlivened by immense imitation roses worn where pennies were put in the era of penny loafers. The high-heeled slippers worn by Louis XIV and his court featured "Louis heels", a term which is still part of the shoemaker's lexicon.

While the ruling class heeled and toed, the peasants of France and the Low Countries wore substantial shoes cut from solid blocks of wood. These *sabots* gave solid protection during the day and later came in handy for sabotaging the property of the rich landowners. Though such practices have long ago been stamped out, wooden clogs can still be seen on feet around the world.

Throughout history those who have done the most walking have shown the best shoe sense. Soldiers in the Crusades, people on pilgrimages, and all the workers and walkers of the world generally avoided the bizarre extreme of the shoe styles. Their footwear was custom made for their feet, usually of soft, flexible leather that was "as comfortable as an old shoe". Even kings realized this and certain of them went back to basics when not on parade. As a contemporary reporter observed in 1689: "King James used to call for his old shoes; they were easiest on his feet."

It was the ordinary foot soldiers and foot sloggers of France who first evolved the idea of stockings. They stuffed thin strips of leather inside their shoes for added warmth and protection. The nobles seized the notion and embellished it by using fabrics such as velvet with gold embroidery. Upper class England at the time of Chaucer wore garish socks of blue and white, or red and white, while most people wore a blanket-cloth variety. The first knitted worsted stockings were invented by an apprentice named William Ryder in 1565. Near the same year Good Queen Bess received a gift of Italian hose knitted from silk and by the end of her reign they were all the rage.

Symbolic shoes

The symbolism of shoes seems innocent enough in the fabled footwear of Cinderella who went from rags to riches to the arms of her prince, via her slippers. Investigations into the origins of the sexual aspects of shoes show just how much the fairy tale censors have toned down the facts.

Back in Greek mythology, Zeus — playing the matchmaker — started his son Hermes, and shoes, down the road to love. Aphrodite, the goddess of love, was being coy with Hermes, so Zeus sent an eagle to steal her shoe. Her search for the missing shoe led her directly into the arms of Hermes.

Shoes came to represent a symbol of female sexuality and sexual submission. The old woman who lived in a shoe and had so many children she didn't know what to do, takes on a new light when examined from this point of view. Folklorists suggest that the old lady's home — her shoe — was really a temple of love and her large brood was the inevitable pre-pill outcome of an overactive sex life.

Many societies introduced shoes into the marriage ceremony. In Anglo Saxon England the father of the bride gave his daughter's shoe to the groom. In India the practice of throwing shoes instead of confetti at a wedding was believed to bring good luck and many children. In Chinese ceremonies the groom burned incense before the shoe of his betrothed who died before marriage, and in the Manchu era a bride gave shoes to her husband-to-be, as well as to all of his brothers, who then had sexual access to her. The Hebrews removed the footwear from a man who refused to marry his dead brother's wife.

When a marriage went on the rocks and her husband began to go astray, a lady in ancient Greece might bring the faithless fellow back by having a witch fumigate his sandals with sulphur while chanting magic incantations. An Arab divorcing his wife might say that she was his ill-fitting slipper and cast her off, while in Germany the wife who put on her husband's slipper on their wedding day would build the foundations for wedded bliss and could look forward to easy labor.

But the symbolism of shoes extended beyond sex, marriage, and birth control. Putting shoes on or off was connected with the idea of ownership in Biblical times. The Egyptians, Assyrians, and Hebrews gave a sandal when property was exchanged. In the ninth Psalm, for instance, the casting of a shoe on the land of Edom was a symbol of possession. It was also in those days that shoes were first removed as a sign of respect. Moses and Joshua were instructed to "put off the shoes from thy feet" on holy ground. The practice continues today in many religions. Moslems remove shoes at the door of the mosque and carry them sole to sole in the left, the unclean hand.

Depending on where one lived and what one did with them, shoes could bring good or bad luck. In Japan, to wear shoes in loos was bad luck, while a poor family in India would protect their house by placing a shoe, heel upward, on top of it. It was also in India that a meteorological magician could bring an end to vicious storms by beating hailstones with a shoe. Persecuted Egyptians might walk all over their enemies by painting a likeness of them in the shoe lining. Anyone suffering from nightmares in Germany solved the problem by placing shoes, the wrong end to, at the head of the bed. Some Germans still believe that it is bad luck to sneeze while putting on shoes, and certain Filipinos think that it is tempting fate to leave a pair of slippers too far apart. Dutch children seek the favors of Saint Nicholas on Christmas Eve by leaving their shoes near the chimney so he will know they are safely tucked in bed. The patron saint of European cobblers is Saint Crispin, an early missionary who made shoes for the poor at night from leather supplied by an angel.

When one's days of earthly walking came to an end and "death greased the boots of its victim" as the old French saying went, shoes sometimes played a part in funerals. The normally barefoot Indian tribes of southern California provided shoes for the dead, as did the people of old Russia who dressed the corpse in new shoes in anticipation of a long journey.

How to choose shoes

Bearing in mind the rocky road of shoes past and considering the infinite implications of the symbolism of shoes, a walker of today might be forgiven for approaching the subject of shoes with some trepidation.

The issue is further complicated by the preponderance of footwear available. In 1629 Thomas Beard, armed with a contract to make shoes for the

Pilgrims, brought the honorable trade of shoemaking to America. By the early nineteenth century he and his kind were replaced by machines which nowadays kick footwear out into the marketplace at a staggering rate. They come in all sizes, shapes, styles and prices, and are geared for every imaginable purpose, but all too seldom for the simple act of walking.

The marketplace of the developed world diligently responds to the phenomenon of contemporary footwear by gobbling the cobbling at a rate of nearly three pairs of shoes per pair of feet every year. Walkers are offered a bewildering assortment of things to put on their feet. However, quantity does not necessarily mean quality and many of the maladies linger on.

Many of the things people put on their feet are still unsuitable for walking.

Publius Syrus, a profound pedestrian from far back in the history of shoes, spoke straight from his feet when he said: "You cannot put the same shoe on every foot." It depends on the why, where, and weather of walking. Everyday, workaday world shoes are fine for everyday, workaday world walking, if they satisfy the basic requirements of the foot. Sandals, the first shoes, walk well enough on short jaunts in warm weather. The best of them have a sole that looks like the bottom of your foot and ties that don't bind excessively. The footwear of runners and joggers, (a walker's first cousins), perform well on pavement. Although designed for speed, they respond nicely to sauntering. Padding helps cushion city shocks and the light weight is less tiring than everyday shoes. They are also suitable for excursions on to grassy surfaces in dry conditions.

For those feet that venture into the rough and tumble of wilderness walking, extra protection is needed to negotiate the rocks, sand, brush, rain, snow, ice, creatures, and other obstacles that may be encountered there. Here, ankles need boots for support and heels and soles need non-skid treads. These boots should have tongues and padding around the top to keep out pebbles, grit, twigs, and living things, and a minimum of seams where they might leak. Mountaineers, desert walkers, hikers, backpackers, and other specialists have their own range of footwear to choose from. Many of these have added options such as insoles, sweat-proofing, and fleece linings for cold weather sorties. Any boots of this type should not extend higher than the ankle and never be so loaded with extras that they do not flex.

Wilderness walkers might bear in mind the effects of tractor-type soles on the trails on which they tread. Environmentalists report that popular trails are now taking on the appearance of well-traveled highways. Softer soled shoes are not only easier to walk in, they also help cushion trails from walkers.

A final word about types of footwear comes from one of the world's great walkers. As a nation, the British probably walk more than most. Ralph Waldo Emerson said: "I find the Englishman to be him of all men who stands firmest in his shoes." Surely John Hillaby must stand firmest of all living Englishmen. Using only foot power, Hillaby has made journeys to Lake Rudolf in northern Kenya, through Britain, and through Europe. His books which describe these treks are among the most entertaining reading on walking; a man with that many miles under his feet is not to be taken lightly. In *Journey Through Britain* he observes: "Footwear is tricky ... Most people advocate stout boots and thick socks. I know of nothing more uncomfortable. They give you a leaden, non-springy stride. You can't trot along in boots. I bought two pairs, broke them in and eventually threw them aside. On a trip across the desert some years ago I wore tennis shoes, but these, I found, are useless in Britain. After trying various kinds of shoes, I settled for an expensive Italian pair with light commando-type soles. They weighed about fifteen ounces each and, when oiled, fitted me like gloves. I had no trouble with shoes."

Material and fit

Leather is best. Because it is flexible, it molds itself to the upper structure of the foot and bends easily at the sole. Because it is porous, leather breathes, allowing fresh air to circulate and cool your foot, while permitting perspiration to seep out which helps keep your foot dry. Because it is durable, it will outlast most other materials. Because it is natural, leather looks and feels good. Because it is tough, it protects the feet against minor collisions; tests have shown that leather soles are four times more resistant to puncture than any other footwear material. Leather works well on the bottom of the sole in tandem with synthetics like rubber or vibram to give a good grip.

The horror of ill-fitting footwear, the major cause of the walking wounded, is illustrated in this two hundred and fifty year old bit of verse from the pen of John Gay, another British walker, writer, and poet.

> *Let firm, well-hammered soles protect thy feet*
> *Through freezing snows, rains and soaking sleet*
> *Should the big last extend the shoe too wide*
> *Each stone will wrench the unwary step aside*
> *The sudden turn may stretch the swelling vein*
> *The cracking joint unhinge or ankle sprain*
> *And when too short thy shoes are worn*
> *Ye'll judge the season by your shooting corns.*

The "big last" referred to in the poem is the first thing you should examine in potential shoes. The last, the wooden or metal model from which shoes are shaped, is what you find when you look at a shoe from the bottom. It should be shaped like the bottom of your foot. All else is style and embellishment and to be avoided in the quest for sensible shoes.

Shun pointed toes unless you want to be able to "judge the season by your shooting corns". Seek a shoe which allows your toes to rest easily on the inner sole so that they are naturally spread. A box toe, in which your toes can wiggle at will, is best. There should be enough room overhead and in front so that your toe joints do not rub too hard against the leather.

Snugness — not tightness — is what to aim for in the rest of the shoe, particularly in the heel, under the arch, and across the instep from the ankle to the ball of the foot. A proper fit provides support but does not bind. Wiggle your heels, arches, and the ball of your foot. Should you encounter any seams, or breaks in seams, consider them as a potential blister.

88

Your arch is as personal as your fingerprint. Make sure the one in your shoe conforms to the one in your foot.

Thou shalt not wear high heels lest "the cracking joint unhinge". Heel height should be slightly higher than the ball of your foot but not so high as to throw your weight forward. The heel rise, the rearmost part of the shoe heel on the inner sole, should meet neatly with the back of your heel, never extending beyond the bulge there. The heel cup, the part that cups around your heel, should nestle nicely into your heel bulge. The heel counter, the rim at the back of the shoe, should be rigid to stabilize your heel but not bite into the Achilles tendon.

Soles should be flexible enough to permit the normal rocking in walking. Test this first by hand, squeezing and bending them smartly. Then stand up and rock around in the shoes. Ideal sole flexibility should allow the front third of your foot to bend as in walking, while being thick enough to help cushion any shocking.

When trying on shoes, wear the socks in which you intend to walk. Socks are the ambassadors of good will between your feet and your shoes. As such, they should be chosen diplomatically, with considerations to both shoe and foot. Wool is a foot's best friend. Heavy wool is warm — wet or dry. Light wool is cool. Wool breathes. It absorbs sweat. It fits better than synthetic fabrics. It doesn't bunch when walking. It wears well. It is natural. It feels good on most feet. For those feet that wool itches, cotton is next best. It, too, is a natural product and it mixes well with wool in socks.

All socks should fit like shoes, snugly, but allowing the foot to flex freely, and with no seams in chafe-prone areas. Many heavy-duty walkers advocate two pairs of socks for added warmth and cushioning. In this case the outer pair should be larger and thicker than the inner. In extreme winter conditions some people resort to a third pair of socks and insoles of felt or hair for more warmth and padding. Once this stage of bundling is reached, the act of walking becomes more like snowshoeing, a pleasant enough pastime on devices built for that purpose, but hard on feet thus encased. Admiral Peary testified to this in his book, *The North Pole* (1910): "We returned from the Pole to Cape Columbia in only sixteen days ... the exhilaration of success lent wings to our sorely battered feet."

Size and cost

Ideally you should buy your shoes in the evening of a dry day. This is because the rigors of walking and standing, as well as humidity, contrive to swell your feet. At the end of a non-humid day they should be back to normal size, but remember to allow for tomorrow's expansion.

Bear in mind the ancient adage of Montaigne: *"A chaque pied, son soulier"* or translated: "To each foot, its shoe." Have *both* your feet measured for length and width because one of them is always larger than the other. You might start with the right foot, which was considered the lucky one in China.

It is self-evident that the heavier you are, the sturdier your shoes should be. When the shoe salesman lays his wares at your feet, pick them up and assess them from the point of view of carrying their weight for many miles. Visualize them taking you on a thousand mile trek. Are they light? More weight means more work in walking. Are they well designed? Serious sporting shoes have sleek and compact styling with no excess frills and bulk. Now try them on for size. Strap yourself into them. Perform the wiggle tests, walk around in them, and try to wear out your welcome if you can before you buy.

Since walking is free, you can afford to spend extra money on your shoes. And, since you usually get what you pay for in footwear, buy the best. All too often in shoes, a penny saved is a foot burned.

CHAPTER EIGHT

"Something old, something new,
Something borrowed, something
blue,
And a lucky sixpence in her shoe."
Anonymous

8

Peripatetic Paraphernalia

A wardrobe for walking in step with the weather and whether to bring along a pack, walking stick, dog, or friend.

One of the joys of the sport of walking is the lack of trappings necessary to participate in it. A body can walk perfectly well, in fact better, outside the restricting confines of a uniform. A spirit can soar to magnificent heights unhampered by the weight of specialized equipment or the limitations imposed by a rule book.

To be absolutely footloose and fancy free a walker needs only a willing body and a landscape to let it loose in. However, various considerations including concrete, climate, and convention dictate the need for a minimum amount of gear. Much of the world that is left to walk in is paved and that pavement is littered with the debris of civilization. This, coupled with the fact that even the little remaining natural world can be hazardous to feet, makes a strong case for a firm foundation of footwear. Beyond that, what you really need for walking is next to nothing.

A walking wardrobe

What you wear while walking should be kept to the bare minimum. Walk naked if you can. One of the main jobs of the skin, after its primary function of containing our innards, is to regulate our body temperature. In hot times the skin accomplishes this by dilating its blood vessels so that more blood comes to the surface for cooling. At the same time the skin secretes perspiration which evaporates and cools the body further. Clothes interfere with this process.

The case for nude walking is supported by Dr. O.G. Edholm, head of the Department of Human Physiology at the National Institute for Medical Research in London. In his words: "In these circumstances, any clothing is a barrier to heat exchange; so in theory complete nudity is the answer." In deference to esthetic and moral reasons, and in consideration of the slings and arrows of insects and plants which cross the walker's path, the doctor allows that "the practical minimum of clothing" should be worn in warm weather. Another benefit of minimal clothing is to give the blood vessels in the skin a workout. They thrive on temperature variations and need the exercise of adapting to those changes in order to be responsive to our health needs.

Choosing clothing is simplified when you bear in mind these basic principles for a walking wardrobe: Keep it light and keep it loose. In hot weather, clothes that are light in color help to reflect the sun's rays. As well as being light and loose, clothing should be permeable and thus able to breathe. Unless clothing breathes, perspiration cannot evaporate. Wool and cotton are the fabrics that do this best because they transmit the moisture from the ends of their fibers like a wick.

Experienced warm weather walkers wear a thin shirt with buttons on collar and sleeves that can be done up or undone in tune with the sun. Wear shorts when you can, but for purposeful striding through rough country, trousers are advisable. Tight jeans may perform beautifully while sitting on a horse, standing around or posing, but are not too practical for walking. Trousers should leave seat and legs free to get on with the job of walking. Corduroy knickers with wool kneesocks are popular in Europe and excellent for walking. The material is strong and reasonably weatherproof and knickered legs give a freedom of movement with no flapping cuffs to drag a walker down.

Most heads are weatherproof and therefore headgear is optional. An average head of hair is

Since most heads are weatherproof, hats are optional.

reasonably rainproof, yet allows the evaporation of sweat; it helps protect against excessive heat loss and guards the skin against sunburn. Scalps provide backup support to the hair and insulate the contents of the skull from the sun's ultraviolet rays. For many years it was thought that too much sun boiled the brain and caused sunstroke! To combat this Victorian walkers sported parasols and travelers in the tropics decked themselves out in pith helmets and neck drapes like those worn by the French Foreign Legion. But hats off to the scientists who discovered that the sun's rays cannot penetrate the cranium. Sun or heatstrokes are caused by the total breakdown of the body's heat-regulating mechanisms and are not related to the overheating of the skull, making portable sunshades unnecessary in most circumstances, although some conditions do call for a hat.

At the other end of the climatic calendar, experiments have shown that twenty percent of the heat of a naked body escapes through the head. Therefore a level-headed walker will wear headgear in cold weather. Elsewhere, heat loss occurs evenly over the body wherever the skin is exposed to the elements. Since the legs account for about a third of the surface area of the body, the torso another third, and because the hands and feet are the last stop on the circulation line, it follows that steps must be taken over your whole body to keep it warm in cold weather walking. The best way to protect a structure from the cold is to insulate it. For the body this means enveloping it in a cocoon of warm and dry air held inside clothes. A normal layer of clothing will trap about fifty pints of air around a body. The more layers there are, the better.

Two thin layers of underwear hold more air than one thin layer. Open weave underwear achieves the same effect in one layer. Wool and other natural fibers trap air better than the more densely woven synthetics. This is not to say that a walker should be surrounded by balloons of hot air. Wool or its breathing counterparts, such as cotton, have a resilience that resists compression and allows molecules of air to be contained between the fibers.

Another shocking thing about synthetics is their tendency to generate static electricity. A walking session in unnatural materials can develop a charge of up to 10,000 volts per square inch — enough to set off explosives.

To keep that valuable warm air inside necessitates the wearing of outerclothes that are wind and waterproof: windproof to keep any breezes from spiriting away the warmth and waterproof because dry clothes keep the heat in. Clothes lose nearly half their insulating value when wet. When choosing outerwear make sure it breathes or trapped perspiration will have you as wet inside as if you were standing under a shower.

Ideally a walker would come equipped with an anatomical thermostat which could be adjusted to fluctuating temperatures but layers of clothing make an effective substitute. Since removing layers of underwear may not always be convenient, shirts and sweaters can take up the task. These items beneath your outerwear can be shed when walking speed generates heat. Conversely they can be donned when you stop for viewing, eating, resting, or such.

Corsets had a detrimental effect on women and walking.

In 1868 the Council of German Women in Stuttgart sought to overthrow the "tyranny and vagaries of fashion" and wear only garments that met "the demands of taste and suitability". Their dress-reform action was preceded by a late eighteenth century book written by a number of doctors. In it these medical men attacked corsets which, they said, caused ninety-seven separate diseases in women. Among them were sleepiness, apoplexy, whooping-cough, consumption and epilepsy — any of which would tend to have a detrimental effect on walking. Though corsets went out with the bustle, girdles persist, and too many tight clothes still cramp a walker's style. (When corsets finally bit the dust in World War I, it was estimated that 28,000 tons of steel were saved, enough to build two battleships.)

A walker's body needs to be free to move. Amelia Jenks Bloomer of New York struck a fine blow for walking women when she threw away the cumbersome hooped petticoats of nineteenth century America and substituted the loose-fitting pantaloon style of undies that were named after her. Yet, even today, many women still struggle into panty girdles in pursuit of a sleek silhouette. Though their anatomy may be thus artificially aided, walking is not. Much better to follow the lead of Mrs. Bloomer and let walking work on the shape. A study in England showed that constricting underwear of various types leads to varicose veins and tight bras can cause neuritis in the arms and fibrositis of the shoulders. Like shoes, bras should permit that which they contain to flex freely. Tight jockey shorts and ummentionables of all types — in fact any ties that bind, lump, or chafe — inhibit circulation and interfere with walking comfort. This applies to gloves and socks as well. Cramped hands and feet prevent proper blood flow which in cold weather predisposes chilblains and frozen extremities.

Bloomers were a breakthrough for lady walkers.

Loose clothing has always been associated with relaxation and tight clothing with discipline and tension. Soldiers gird up their loins to do battle. Tight collars and ties might help arm businessmen for their confrontations but comfortable knitwear and open necked shirts are better for the serenity of the open road. The soothing effects of loose garments were pointed out by a nineteenth century physician in Edinburgh. Dr. Andrew Combe recommended the wearing of unconfining clothes so that "every movement of the body gives a gentle stimulus to the cutaneous vessels and nerves, which assists their actions and maintains their function and health."

In a nutshell then, when choosing a wardrobe for walking, less is best, and it should be loose. Wear as little as the weather warrants, for a body mummified in too much clothing is sealed off physically and spiritually from the world through which it walks. Although taking an unkind cut at a lady's physique and speaking from a non-walking vantage point, Frances Cornford captured the essence of this idea in *To a Fat Lady Seen from the Train:*

> *O why do you walk through the fields in gloves,*
> *Missing so much and so much?*
> *O fat white woman whom nobody loves,*

Why do you walk through the fields in gloves
When the grass is soft as the breast of doves
And shivering sweet to the touch?

Tripping the light fantastic

A "gentleman of the road" with all his worldly possessions.

When outfitting themselves with aids and accessories, walkers might do well to take a tip from tramps — or "gentlemen of the road" as they were called in England — and the young men of song and story who set off down the road to seek their fortunes. For life afoot these folk managed to bundle up all their worldly possessions in a small kerchief. One such fellow was Englishman Thomas Coryat, who took to the open road from his home in Odcombe, Somerset. A "Panegyrick Verse" (panegyric: laudatory) from his book, *Coryat's Crudities,* published in 1611, tells what he took on his journey to Venice, during which he averaged twenty-one miles a day:

He launched forth his hulke:
The sides whereof were heard to groane
No less than twenty miles and one
Under his grievous bulke.
Then either without scrippe or bagge
He usde his ten-toes for a nagge
From Venice for to hie.
Thorough thicke, and thorough thinne
Untill he came unto his Inne,
His winged heeles did flie.

Unquestionably "winged heeles flie" better without the encumbrance of "scrippes" (satchels) or "bagges" but sacks, whether they be knap, ruck or pack, can be useful for excursions both epic and everyday. Your walking ambitions will determine the size and scope of your pack but consider first a simple solution — pockets. Several varieties of sporting coats and vests feature stylings where pockets and pouches predominate. Among these are fisherman's, hunter's, and photographer's vests as well as the traditional hacking jacket. These will provide cargo accommodation for anything short of an overnight jaunt. A well-chosen belt, with loops and fasteners from which to dangle shed clothing and the like, is another solution.

The pack should be durable, weatherproof, and —

in deference to the back on to which it will be strapped — as light in weight as possible. Straps should be broad, flat, and padded to protect the collar bones and shoulder blades on which it will ride. They should also be adjustable so as to prevent restricting the shoulder and arm movements of the walking stride. The pack should be worn high on the back with soft items against the shoulders. A pack worn too low will upset the center of gravity. For this reason your sack should be evenly packed with heavier objects at the top and middle, next to the back, which promotes stability and helps prevent sway. Backpacks with metal frames are for back-packing, a pursuit which a walker may venture into, but an activity that has its own special rules and requirements.

A city walk, or a short walk anywhere, requires no more baggage than perhaps a wallet for survival. However, there are certain trappings for the trail that can enhance a longer walk. A short list of these might include maps and compasses for unknown territory; binoculars and field guides for identifying flora and fauna; a camera and/or notebook for recording encounters; a pedometer for measuring miles (although most of them are inaccurate); a flask and other first aid items for emergencies; insect repellent and sunglasses for those eventualities; a change of socks for the feet; a book of poems for the soul; and food and drink to nourish the walking body. For his seven hundred mile walk from Toul, in northeastern France, to Rome the contents of Hilaire Belloc's pack consisted of "a large piece of bread, half a pound of smoked ham, a sketch book, two Nationalist papers, a quart of the wine of Brule, a needle, some thread and a flute."

Regarding food, casual nibbling is the order of the day for casual walking. Heavy meals make for heavy steps. Needless to say a wise walker will resist junk food as he would avoid synthetic shoes. Sensible sandwiches, cheese, hard cooked eggs, nuts, raisins, and fruit provide energy and are easily carried, outside and inside the body. Long distance walkers need fat, (butter thickly spread on sandwiches will provide this), and plenty of liquids. On his walk through England, John Hillaby drank three pints of ale at lunch and a similar quantity, sometimes more, at night. One of the joys of walking in Britain is the liquid refreshment available at pubs. Walkers elsewhere can make do with a canteen of water.

Before you cram your shiny new pack full to the brim, remember that everything you put there should enhance and not impede your journey. Don't take it all with you in order to get away from it all.

The cult of canes

The idea of staffs, canes, or walking sticks is probably directly descended from the clubs wielded by the first walkers. When Jesus sent his disciples out to spread the good word He "commanded them that they should take nothing for their journey, save a staff only; no scrip, no bread, no money in their purse." He did allow that they "be shod with sandals" but presumably their staffs were all they needed to give them "power over unclean spirits". The spread of Christianity indicates that their walking sticks served them well.

These Biblical staffs mentioned in Chapter 6 of St. Mark's Gospel were probably of the shepherd's crook variety. They measured about four feet eight inches in length and were handy for managing the flock as well as fending off danger. The fact that the Lord carried a rod or staff was particularly reassuring as noted in the twenty-third Psalm: "Yea, though I walk through the valley of the shadow of death, I will fear no evil: for Thou art with me, Thy rod and staff they comfort me."

Not long after Sherwood Forest had echoed with the sounds of the celebrated quarter staff joust between Robin Hood and Little John, the size and shape of walking weaponry shrank to sticks and canes. Though they were cloaked in all manner of disguises, they continued to be thought of primarily for defensive purposes. In seventeenth century England walking sticks were made from assorted materials including ivory, bone, ebony, bamboo, whangee, and whampoo as well as pear, cherry, tobacco, vine, and banana woods. They might have been bejeweled with diamonds, gold, sapphires, emeralds, amber, or jade. Many of them contained secret swords, daggers, or guns. One of these weapon sticks from 1770 bore this self-description:

My silver head contains some lead
And a large amount of tin
To crack a malefactor's head
Or a true blade lies within.

No self-respecting walker would venture forth without a trusty stick in hand. One such fictional gentleman, Mr. Jogglebury Crowdey, developed a fetish for his "Gibbey Sticks", as he called them. Robert Surtees wrote about his adventures in *Mr. Sponge's Sporting Tour,* a best-seller of 1853. On Jogglebury's jaunts through the English countryside he mentally marked out branches for their stick potential. He returned late at night to chop them down, took them back to his workshop, and transformed them into thousands of walking sticks with carved tops in the form of kings, queens, bishops, and other notables as well as animals, birds, and reptiles.

Cane peddlers enabled bipeds to become tripods.

Eventually the walking sticks of Jogglebury Crowdey and his ilk came to be wielded as badges of office. In his *Theory of the Leisure Class,* Thorstein Veblen wrote: "The walking stick serves the purpose of an advertisement that the bearer's hands are employed otherwise than in useful effort, and it therefore has utility as an evidence of leisure." There were black dress canes for evening strolls, usually of ebony with massive silver tops, and ivory handled sticks for the ladies. Sporting sticks became all the rage. Some of them blossomed into brollies for wet weather walking, and others — shooting and fishing sticks — folded out into little chairs. Certain canes concealed other items that catered to their owner's surreptitious habits including poker dice and whiskey. A musically inclined walker could carry a cane that doubled as a flute, and the military adopted service and swagger sticks marked according to rank.

All sorts of exotic and trick sticks became available. One magic wand, made from the penis of a bull, turned and polished to a high degree so that it was as translucent as amber, was intended to bestow fertility on the walker who wielded it, as well as the crops of his fields through which he strode.

Although walking sticks have become rather less fanciful objects today, they serve a useful purpose in encouraging a free-swinging stride, are handy for sweeping aside wayward vegetation and their anti-canine properties should not be overlooked. John Hillaby said it in his *Journey Through Europe*. During his traverse through the Vosges region of France he used a "bone-dry piece of Arolla pine, near six foot in length and towards the base as thick as my arm" to fend off "an apple-headed cur scarce larger than a ferret". He christened his stick "Willibrord" but threw it away after it had served his purpose, holding that "arms are meant to be swung to increase momentum," and that "the burden of protection seemed greater than the hazards of walking unarmed, and I next to never carried a staff again ... a walker is a biped not a tripod."

Walking the dog

The practice of walking with dogs began about 5000 years ago in Egypt and China and there are still many arguments in support of the company of "man's best friend" on a walk. In his book of essays, *A Man and His Dog,* Thomas Mann described how his Bashan added enjoyment to a morning walk, the dog's exuberant pleasure enhancing his own. "You

Man has walked with his "best friend" for 5000 years.

are the right royal lord of the mad hunter yonder who is making another jump across the fence out of sheer joy." Bashan loved to leap across the fence, and did so again and again, returning each time to receive his master's praise.

It can be fun to play fetch with Fido in the park and often a canine companion will willingly serve as a useful introduction to fellow dog fanciers. If Fido happens to be an exotic breed he becomes a walking status symbol providing ego-boosting benefits. A large dog straining on the end of a leash can do wonders for a walker's courage on late night trips down dark alleys. Many walkers who are barked at by their peers or relatives during the day find release by dominating their dogs. For these people, a submissive dog serves to raise them at least one notch in life's pecking order.

On the other side of the coin, and often on the sole of a walker's shoe, walked dogs can mean a mess of trouble. In London 500,000 dogs deposit about one million pints of urine and seventy tons of feces every day on the city's parks and streets. A walker dodging dog droppings is likely to develop ambivalent feelings about the 280,000 dogs in Tokyo, 300,000 in Los Angeles, 700,000 in New York, and over a million in Mexico City. Other statistics show that walkers should be wary of both ends of dogs. "He cannot be a gentleman who loveth not a dog" begins to wear a bit thin when one considers that New York's toll of dog bites runs at something like 75,000 a year and 1.5 percent of all hospital emergency admissions in America are for walking wounds inflicted by dogs.

Steps are being taken around the world to curb dog dirtying. Many communities insist that those walking dogs carry "pooper-scoopers". In Holland street signs read "Don't let your dog foul the pavement" beneath a pictograph of a dog doing just that. The authorities in some cities in the south of France have taken a more direct approach with signs that show the dog serenely looking the other way while its owner, on the end of a leash, emulates the dirty deed usually performed by dogs.

Dogs are something like the sacred cows of India.

Walking the dog is sometimes a mixed blessing.

It has even been suggested that the spelling of dog backwards indicates the degree of reverence and devotion in which many hold these animals. But the fact remains that in Britain for instance running dogs are responsible for nine road deaths or serious injuries every week and they kill more than ten thousand sheep and poultry each year. The chances of a walker having to deal with an irate dog asserting its territorial rights are very high. In Britain the ratio of dogs to humans is 1 to 9.4, in France 1 to 6.8, and in America 1 to 6.2.

The right to the delights of dogs in walking cannot be denied but they should be under their master's control at all times. Walkers and dogs should be obedient to the code of the road and respect the rights of dogless pedestrians. "Heel, Rover" and "Down, Sport" applies to both master and mutt.

The company of walkers

There you stand with the world at your feet, a walker on the threshold of adventure, sartorially splendid in your light and loose clothing, and with or without a pack, cane, or dog. Is something missing? Or is it someone? Sooner or later a walker must decide whether or not to walk alone. Loneliness is not the prerogative of the long distance runner. The more gregarious walkers probably won't lift a foot without a friend but the implications of walking with companions are worth investigating.

We actually walk differently in crowds than we do in the wide open spaces. Normal body sway of about one and a half inches to the left and right soars to almost four inches when we wade through packs of our fellow men and women. Partly this is due to the pelvis executing avoidance measures in order to avoid collisions but it is also a subconscious attempt to thwart the invasion of our privacy. Whenever anyone else enters into this hallowed space, walking becomes a different sport.

Down through the years many well known walkers have weighed the pros and cons of walking companions. The ultimate decision is, of course, an individual one, but a look at their varied opinions may serve to shed some light on a controversy which

104

is still very much alive.

She is pretty to walk with,
And witty to talk with,
And pleasant, too, to think on.

So thought Sir John Suckling. Robert Browning Hamilton, on the other hand, countered with:

I walked a mile with Pleasure
She chattered all the way.
But left me none the wiser
For all she had to say.

It would seem that:

Walking and talking
Rhyme
Most of the time
But aren't necessarily
In harmony.

Lest the feminine references in the preceding quotations be singled out for sexual bias, Emily Brontë had strong feelings about walking alone:

I'll walk where my own nature would be
leading.
It vexes me to choose another guide.

And to counterbalance that sentiment, some words from Edgar Guest:

I'd rather see a sermon than hear one any day;
I'd rather one should walk with me than merely
tell the way.

Some people, like Bliss Carman, prefer to walk in the company of God:

I took a day to search for God,
And found Him not. But as I trod
By rocky ledge, through woods untamed,
Just where one scarlet lily flamed,
I saw His footprint in the sod.

Amos, the ancient Jewish prophet, enquired: "Can two walk together, except they be agreed?"

Many of the world's great wordsmiths were prolific walkers. Samuel Taylor Coleridge and the Wordsworths, William and his sister Dorothy, walked hundreds of miles together, arguing and discussing what they intended to write. Coleridge said they were "three persons and one soul". William Hazlitt, the critic and essayist who walked with Coleridge, disagreed with walking and talking at the same time: "I like solitude."

Hazlitt and Sir Walter Raleigh seem to have been solitary walkers. Sir Walter may have been chivalrous when he laid down his coat for Queen Elizabeth, but later he became something less than gregarious, judging by this item from his *Wishes of an Elderly Man:*

I wish I loved the Human Race;
I wish I loved its silly face;
I wish I liked the way it walks;
I wish I lived the way it talks;
And when I'm introduced to one
I wish I thought What Jolly Fun!

Ralph Waldo Emerson said: "There are two companions with one or other of whom 'tis desirable to go out on a tramp. One is an artist, that is, who has an eye for beauty . . . you shall see through his eyes; and if they be of great discernment, you will learn wonderful secrets . . . The other is a naturalist, for the reason that it is much better to learn the elements of geology, of botany, or ornithology and astronomy by word of mouth from a companion than dully from a book." But he added words of caution: "Good observers have the manners of trees and

Emerson preferred to walk with an artist, a naturalist, or a dog.

animals, their patient good sense, and if they add words, 'tis only when words are better than silence. But a loud singer, or a story-teller, or a vain talker profanes the river and forest, and is nothing like so good company as a dog ..."

CHAPTER NINE

"News of battle! — news of battle!
Hark! 'tis ringing down the street;
And the archways and the pave-
ment
Bear the clang of hurrying feet."
William Aytoun

9

Marching to a Different Drum

The behavior of walkers, how everyone does it differently, and a look at what beats the drum.

Beyond the basic physiological factors that control the way we walk, there are certain phenomena — psychological and illogical — that determine whether we amble, march, meander, mince, sashay, saunter, shuffle, strut, swagger, waddle, or wiggle along through life. The variety of individual styles, often as personal as a fingerprint, is what makes walker-watching such a fascinating pastime.

The portable buffer zone

The physical space that we occupy on earth, examined from an overhead perspective, can be measured by body depth and shoulder breadth. Large numbers of human factor studies have established a maximum body depth dimension of thirteen inches with shoulder breadth averaging about twenty-one inches. To allow us room to turn around freely, to carry personal articles and to account for normal body sway, the studies have granted us an eighteen by twenty-four inch body ellipse in which to walk. Thus, wherever we go, each of us carries an elliptical umbrella occupying the equivalent of 2.3 square feet of space.

Everyone marches to a different drum.

From this private, portable buffer zone we perceive our surroundings through sight, sound, smell, touch, and taste. To allow these senses to

We carry an eighteen by twenty-four inch elliptical umbrella with us when we walk.

interact efficiently with the environment and for peace of mind, we require approximately twenty-five square feet of space. Radiating out from our buffer zone are varying distances inside that twenty-five square foot ideal that have been categorized as intimate, personal, social, and public boundaries. The computation of these distances may alter with the density of population. For instance, people accustomed to crowds usually have greater tolerances. However, regardless of the number of feet involved, we behave differently in each of these areas and subconsciously take steps to adjust to them.

The public distance, measuring from twenty-five feet to within twelve feet of our buffer zone, is a no man's land. Within this range our sensory contact with people and objects is limited, enabling us to stroll along freely without any appreciable change in normal walking style. Threats to our personal space are minimal; if we see trouble coming we can easily take evasive action and literally or figuratively cross to the other side of the street. If we wish to communicate from this distance we have to exaggerate and stylize our speech and posture — something which every good stage actor knows. Voices must be raised and body stance emphasized. Sometimes, to gain the attention of others in the public distance or if we feel intimidated by them watching us, we tend to focus on our stride. Since walking is a reflex action, this can upset the natural rhythm, disturb normal coordination, and may result in an ungainly gait or even a pratfall.

At the social distance, which occupies an area of from four to twelve feet around us, behavioral changes intensify. It is here that the circle of personal involvement and potential vulnerability begins. It was in this same space that combatants with foils did their parrying and thrusting in the swashbuckling era. During casual social intercourse we are also *en garde.* Most formal business activity and conversation is conducted at seven to twelve feet within the social distance. We use a sensory "fencing" process to evaluate situations in this area and it is possible to achieve arm's length contact if so desired. While this is going on, many walkers can be observed as they think on their feet. They might sidle slyly, tiptoe timidly, march menacingly, or stride confidently, depending on their personality and reaction to the situation.

The personal distance, beginning at four feet and coming to within two and a half feet of our buffer zone, is our circle of trust. Anyone treading here comes by invitation only. Should they venture into it without our permission, we tend to feel threatened.

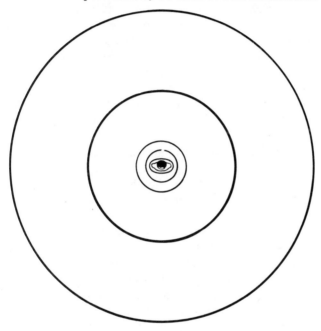

Twenty-five, twelve, four, and two and a half foot distances make up our portable buffer zone.

Pedestrians walking in crowds protect this area by adjusting their pace and speed to avoid collisions and unwanted contact. In dense traffic our normal body sway of one and a half inches to the right and left becomes exaggerated to four inches on either side, throwing us off balance and transforming walking into a tightrope walker's gravity-defying dance. Our senses reveal personal details of those we meet during these encounters — if we like what we see, smell, and hear, we can invite them in for a touch or taste. Should we extend an invitation and it is refused, we feel rebuffed. In some cases this defeat can cause the confidence to disappear from our step and bring on a case of the shuffles.

113

The final space around our buffer zone, anything closer than two and a half feet, is the intimate distance. What we experience in this highly charged area can raise our spirits or our hackles. In transporting our portable buffer zone around, our feet have intimate contact with the earth at all times. The walking stride transmits the positives and negatives of the landscape to our psyche and our sensory organs are turned up full volume to perceive that which we encounter in our intimate distance. Sometimes contact here is too close for comfort and we get a distorted view, much the same as looking at a painting from close up. The brush strokes predominate. Conversely, if we find the painting pleasant to look at from a distance, bringing it into our intimate area for a close up view can add to our enjoyment of it and give it more depth and dimension.

With people, as with paintings, if we like what we see, we slow our movements down or stop completely to further heighten the experience. When faced with a painting, person, or other object that we don't care to inspect close up, we react by subconsciously allowing our intimate distance to shrink, thereby protecting our privacy. Our walking stride tightens up and loses identity as we attempt to hide from, or avoid, an unwanted confrontation. We become tense and the natural pendular motions of our legs are constricted, leading to inefficient walking. This factor, coupled with the desire to flee, *Crowds cause us to* helps to account for the pained expressions of *walk differently.* pedestrians in rush hour traffic.

Psyche and style

We need elbow room, mental and physical, to think and move freely, but other factors govern the way we walk. As our minds and feet jockey for position in life our steps follow suit, so that our walking style often reflects our emotions.

High spirits can inject a spring into the step and perpetually happy people seem to bounce along like a rubber ball. Their elation causes them to emphasize the rising-up-on-the-toe sequence of walking so that they move forward in a jerky, devil-may-care parabola.

When our universe is unfolding as it should and we have our twenty-five square feet or more to play with, we can stroll along casually. This form of slow walking is usually accomplished at a rate of about one step per second with frequent pauses for a look or a talk. The average walking pace is two steps per second, or about three miles per hour, but in strolling it is the journey, not the arrival, that matters.

Another product of a happy or contented state of mind is the saunter — a nirvana state of walking. Henry David Thoreau praised those who had a genius for sauntering and discussed its origins in his essay, *On Walking* "... which word is beautifully derived from idle people who roved about the country, in the Middle Ages, and asked charity, under pretense of going *à la Sainte Terre,* to the Holy Land, till the children exclaimed, 'There goes a Sainte-Terrer,' a Saunterer, a Holy-Lander. They who never go to the Holy Land in their walks, as they pretend, are indeed mere idlers and vagabonds; ... they who do go there are saunterers in the good sense, such as I mean. Some, however, would derive the word from *sans terre,* without land or home, which, therefore, in the good sense, will mean, having no particular home, but equally at home everywhere. For this is the secret of successful sauntering. He who sits still in a house all the time may be the greatest vagrant of all; but the saunterer, in the good sense, is no more vagrant than the meandering river, which is all the while sedulously seeking the shortest course to the seas."

Heavy hearts make heavy feet as Shakespeare noted:

> *Jog on, jog on the footpath way,*
> *And merrily hent the stile-a;*
> *A merry heart goes all the day,*
> *Your sad tires in a mile-a.*

In *The Exhilarations of the Road* John Burroughs pointed out the difficulties of walking with a heavy heart: "The human body is a steed that goes freest and longest under a light rider, and the lightest of all riders is a cheerful heart. Your sad, or morose, or embittered, or preoccupied heart settles heavily into the saddle, and the poor beast, the body, breaks down the first mile. Indeed, the heaviest thing in the world is a heavy heart."

Burroughs goes on to mention another state of mind or heart that can affect the way we walk: "Next to [a heavy heart] the most burdensome to the walker is a heart not in perfect sympathy and accord with the body — a reluctant or unwilling heart." A deeply preoccupied mind or heavy heart can lead a walker astray. An example of this is the pacing performance put on by lecturers, teachers, and instructors involved in improving the minds of others. They often accompany their teachings with a rhythmical pacing back and forth. Normal walking requires next-to-no concentration, but when the mind is totally involved, a wavering walk can result. When the teacher/pacer reaches the absent-minded professor stage, steps begin to falter with indecision and pace can deteriorate into a stumbling shambles. This happened to Steffano Guazzo, an Italian heavy-thinker/pacer of the sixteenth century: "Going with my feete sometime thither whyther, I go not with my heart."

Impatience, consternation, and confinement are other causes of pacing. Prisoners in cells, although they may have their token twenty-five square feet of ideal space, object strongly to the walls around it and react by pacing for hours on end. Eventually mental fetters of this type can reduce pacing to a shuffle where there is no heel-to-toe action and the feet are hardly raised off the ground.

Certain social encounters can create other ways of

walking. When we wish to sidestep a difficult situation, or sidle up to a potentially pleasant one, we sometimes employ a sideways shuffle or crab-walk. Voyeurs, spies, and others in need of stealth often use a tiptoe approach. This method of locomotion, with only the toes and the ball of the foot in contact with the ground, is quieter than any other.

Marching, the most aggressive form of walking, is sometimes done by civilians as well as the military. If we wish to make a strong point we will "march right up to someone" in no uncertain terms. The marching pace with its lengthened stride, balanced by a stronger swinging of the arms, creates self-confidence and helps tame difficult terrain. It is also useful for putting many miles under the belt as well as putting people in their place. When performed with a stiff-legged kicking action, marching becomes a goose-step, the spectacle of which tends to be even more intimidating.

Past histories and emotional scars are often reflected in walking style. A teenager who grew faster than his or her peers and attempted to disguise the fact by slumping and slouching, may continue to walk that way as an adult. Once-fat people, even after obliterating their obesity, sometimes waddle along as if they were still pushing an expanded waistline ahead of them.

Some walk-watchers feel that the differences in international mentalities can be detected in walking styles. Americans visiting other countries are said to stride more purposefully and aggressively than the natives, their pioneering attitudes and frontier conquering spirit inherent in their walk. Traditionally the British, more than any other nation, have walked for pleasure. John Burroughs felt that this could be seen in the way they walked: "It is indeed astonishing with what ease and hilarity the English walk. To an American it seems a kind of infatuation." Collectively, the effects of thousands of years of concentrated walking and marching gives Europeans a more guarded gait, although when they let their guard down, the individual nationalities are thought to have certain characteristics. Italians are

Do the English walk with "a kind of infatuation"?

supposed to walk with gusto, the French with style, the Germans with precision, the Dutch with deliberation, the Spanish with dignity, and the Scandinavians without inhibition.

Sex, and the choreography of walkers

Reaction to the opposite sex plays a role in the way we walk. One research study, using hidden cameras in crowded shopping centers, showed that men and women behave differently when they pass by one another closely. Seventy-five percent of the men turned their bodies towards the women, eleven percent turned away, while fourteen percent were neutral. Sixty-two percent of the women turned their bodies away from the men, seventeen percent turned towards them and twenty-one percent didn't seem to care one way or another.

A walker seeking to attract the sexual attention of another will strut or sashay, as the case may be, in a manner quite different from his or her normal way of walking. In this ritual mating dance, male strides lengthen, chests jut out, stomachs suddenly become flat, and individual interpretations of macho mannerisms predominate. Female steps take on a more dainty air than normal, breasts and other anatomical attributes are accentuated, and the unique female pelvic rotation movement is often exaggerated. In several Latin American countries the opportunity for the sexes to strut their stuff is provided in the evening *paseo*. Here the eligible young girls parade around the town square in one direction with the available males circulating around them in the opposite direction. Although less formalized, variations on the *paseo* theme are acted out by promenading persons in every society.

The causes of many of contemporary society's ills could probably be found by sifting through the footprints left behind by the passing parade. Trying to transport our buffer zones, psyches, and sexual traits safely through the crowded footpaths of life is tough enough. To have others tag along — whether our desire or theirs — only complicates matters. Walking in tandem or within a group sends locomotive mechanisms haywire. With everyone marching to a different drum, the effort of matching up strides and mentalities serves to derange normally placid souls. Armies solve this problem by marching in unison; the rest of us are left to mill about in straggling disorder, to-ing and fro-ing, and hopping, skipping and jumping, as individual walking styles defy conformity.

There is one common experience shared by walkers the world over. This exasperating and embarrassing little event occurs when we meet another walker in a corridor, doorway, or street. Usually our collision-avoiding system manages to anticipate oncomers and we pass safely by without contact. Occasionally something goes amiss, no one knows why, and the ensuing dance of deviation can be amusing to all but the unwilling partners. In this tangled tango, walker A moves to the left and walker B moves to the right which brings them face to face and toe to toe. Sensing the mistake simultaneously, both A and B dosey-do in opposite directions, only to be confronted with each other again. The *pas de deux* might continue for a third or fourth time until they reach a standstill. Now they pause while each waits for the other to pass. This standoff is usually resolved by A and B dancing off in totally different directions or when one of them asks or gestures the other to go first. Musical accompaniment for this choreography often takes the form of mumbled apologies and clucking noises made by both parties.

The theory of "Gaitology"

Gait, the term used to describe our manner of walking, includes carriage, rhythm, and speed. Our gait is closely integrated with our personality. Formative years are spent adapting and adjusting to heredity and environment. They superimpose themselves on our potential and we draw from them traits that are revealed in our speech, handwriting, and way of walking. Between the ages of twelve and twenty our speech stabilizes into a particular style of intonation and accent, our penmanship takes on distinctive characteristics, and our gait comes of age.

A person's gait is described variously as being noble and proud or meek and mild with variations such as a measured gait that attracts respect, or a slow gait that appears affected. "By her gait one knew the goddess", said Publius Vergilius Maro (Virgil) in the *Aeneid,* his epic poem of the Roman people. Two thousand years later young ladies seeking to become goddesses have their gaits transformed in modeling schools.

The graphic achievement of our upper limbs — handwriting — closely parallels that of our lower limbs — walking. Since graphologists can determine personality traits from the vigor of downstrokes or neglected punctuation, it may be that a "gaitologist" can draw similar conclusions from the way we walk. Many of us subconsciously perform this kind of analysis on the people we meet, as did the French tragic poet, Jean Racine, who protested against "a guide who approaches you with a timid gait".

A hundred years after Racine's time, Honoré de Balzac, the realist novelist, put forward a theory of "gaitology". Taking time out from his *Comédie Humaine,* a long series of novels in which he attempted to depict the whole of nineteenth century French society, he wrote a book entitled *Theory of Gait.* In it he observed: "The Parisian woman has a genius for gait" and proceeded to analyze the strides

"The Parisian woman has a genius for gait."

of his countrymen and women from a personality point of view. The practice of "gaitology" is not popular today but to revive it might serve to illuminate the crystal balls through which we examine *homo sapiens*. There may be a place for footshrinkers as well as headshrinkers in our society.

To take the idea a step further, some graphologists believe that certain negative character traits can be modified by deliberately changing a person's writing style. Thus a "gaitologist" should be able to cure personality defects by altering the manner of walking. Instead of a session on a couch, a patient with an awkward or timid gait might be instructed to march around the office to perfect a more assertive or virile personality. Armies have controlled behavior in this way for centuries by putting out-of-step recruits through endless marching drills. The effect is to transform them into fighting men, through discipline and the subordination of personality variances, by making everyone march to the same drum.

CHAPTER TEN

"A man's walking is a succession of falls."
Old Proverb

10

Scientific Walking

Observing treadmill trudgers and guinea pig plodders under the microscope to unravel the mysteries of walking.

Da Vinci wondered if walkers might be used to power a military engine.

Down through the centuries the subject of walking has intrigued people in many walks of life. Leonardo da Vinci was the first to examine the topic in depth. The Italian painter, sculptor, architect, engineer, man of science, and writer of prose and verse needed all of his considerable talents in those fields to do justice to the many facets of walking. Da Vinci's successors enlisted the aid of many marvelous machines and amazing apparatuses to delve into the secrets of human locomotion.

After da Vinci, the next walk-watcher of note was a countryman of his, Signor Borelli. In 1680 he published the first book devoted entirely to the hows, whys, and wherefores of humanity afoot. *De*

Moto Animalium served as the definitive book on walking for one hundred and ninety-three years.

Then came E.J. Marey, an inventive Frenchman, who put his ear to the ground and his eye to a camera to produce his book, *The Animal Machine,* in 1873. As well as making a significant contribution to the store of scientific knowledge of walking, Marey stumbled upon a discovery which might have made him a candidate for an Academy Award.

He began his research by using a little horse sense. At that time in France, a wise horse dealer would have the animal in question clip-clop around on cobblestones before making a decision. In this way his practiced ear could detect any deficiencies in the way the horse walked. Marey felt that this would be useful in his studies of human gait, so he invented shoes that were wired for sound. Thus shod, his guinea pig walkers marched around gathering sonic data on a hand-held recording cylinder which was connected to a dynamometric inner chamber in the shoes.

After perfecting these "walkie-talkies", Monsieur Marey's next step was to develop movies for studying movement. To capture the series of sequential events that occur in the walking cycle, Marey erected an elaborate set worthy of a Hollywood sound stage. He began with a black backdrop in front of which the actors in his drama paraded back and forth in costumes which blacked out those parts of their anatomy not involved in the study of the moment. Parallel to this, Marey constructed a miniature railway on the tracks of which trundled along a photographic darkroom wherein the director sat snapping away behind his still camera. Marey christened his process chrono-photography. Later inventors, tinkering with this train of thought, ran the series of individual photographs together to create cinematography.

In his introduction to *The Footpath Way,* an anthology for walkers published in Britain in 1911, Hilaire Belloc discussed the feat of walking. He saw it as a play in several acts in the comedy/drama of life:

"Well, all that business of walking that you are

"Walkie-talkies" provided new insights into walking.

looking at is a piece of extraordinarily skillful trick-acting, such that were the animal not known to do it you would swear he could never be trained to it by any process, however lengthy, or however minute, or however strict. This is what happens when a man walks: first of all he is in stable equilibrium, though the arc of stability is minute ... and you may say of a man so standing, even with his feet well spread, that he is already doing a fine athletic feat.

"But wait a moment: he desires to go, to proceed, to reach a distant point, and instead of going on all fours, where equilibrium would indeed be stable, what does he do? He deliberately lifts one of his supports off the ground, and sends his equilibrium to the devil; at the same time he leans a little forward so as to make himself fall towards the object he desires to attain ... What you really do, man, when you want to get to that distant place (and let this be a parable to all adventure and of all desire) is to take an enormous risk, the risk of coming down bang and breaking something; you lift one foot off the ground and, as though that were not enough, you deliberately throw your center of gravity forward so that you begin to fall.

"That is the first act of the comedy.

"The second act is that you check your fall by bringing the foot which you had swung into the air down upon the ground again.

"That you would say was enough of a bout. Slide the other foot up, take a rest, get your breath again and glory in your feat. But not a bit of it! The moment you have got that loose foot of yours on the firm earth, you use the impetus of your first tumble to begin another one. You get your center of gravity by the momentum of your foot going well forward of the foot that has found the ground, you lift the other foot without a care, you let it swing in the fashion of a pendulum, and you check your second fall in the same manner as you checked your first; and even after that second clever little success you do not bring your feet both firmly to the ground to recover yourself before the next venture: you go on with the business, get your center of gravity forward of the foot that is now on the ground, swinging the other beyond it like a pendulum, stopping your third catastrophe, and so on, and you have come to do all this so that you think it is the most natural thing in the world!"

Belloc knew his subject well, having made a personal religious pilgrimage from England to Rome via footpower. For studying walking technically, scientists continued along the route established by Marey. To eliminate the need for laying miles of railway track, they constructed treadmills which allowed them to observe walkers in a confined area. To conduct experiments, walkers were put into harness and wired with electrodes which recorded movements, and laden with tubes into which they breathed. Pulleys, levers, brakes, springs, and tension devices enabled the treadmills to be adjusted to simulate all kinds of walking conditions. Today, more sophisticated versions of these artificial footpaths continue to update the data on walking.

With treadmills humming in laboratories all around the western world it is not surprising that a

Endless treadmill studies have shown the walking body to be more complex than any treadmill.

variety of scientific opinion prevails. For instance the word "walking" is currently defined as meaning:

- an alternation of the lower extremities.

- a translatory motion of the whole brought about by the angular motion of some of its parts.

- an alternating loss and recovery of balance.

- a dynamic equilibrium in which the center of gravity permanently overtakes and passes the base of support in a sort of free-fall forward.

- an alternative falling forward and catching of the center of gravity by opposite legs.

All of these descriptions are accurate but individually biased according to the specialty of the scientists involved. The varying points of view also serve to indicate the complexity of the subject. When the results of all the studies are averaged, a clearer picture of the act of walking emerges, as does one indisputable truth: the most marvelous machine of all, more complex than any of the contraptions devised to study it, is the human body as it walks.

The walking cycle

A complete walking cycle is from heel contact to the next heel contact of the same foot. Within the cycle each leg alternates between a supporting phase and a swinging phase.

The supporting phase starts with the heel strike of the leg extended in front of the body with the center of gravity behind that foot. There are two forces being exerted on this foot — one horizontal and forward against the ground, and the other vertical and down against the ground. The first force slows the forward motion of the body and the latter force stops the fall of the center of gravity. As the foot rocks forward from heel to toe, the center of gravity moves directly above the foot where the vertical force is at a maximum and the horizontal force is at zero. Next, the center of gravity moves ahead of the foot reducing the vertical force to zero and exerting the horizontal force in a backward direction. This latter force reaches a maximum just before the ball of the foot leaves the ground and because it is greater than the vertical force, forward motion is maintained. The sources of motion during this supporting phase come from the momentum of the body and the contraction of the muscles in the supporting leg.

The swinging phase of the walking cycle starts immediately after the push off by the ball of the foot. It begins with flexion at the hip, then further flexion at the knee and ankle. These flexions have two effects: they shorten the length of the leg so it can clear the ground, and they make the leg easier to move by bringing its own center of gravity closer to the point of rotation. After the foot has passed under the body, the knee begins to extend but the hip continues to flex and extend, which slows down the leg. The heel strikes the ground before the toe because the ankle is flexed. The sources of motion during this swinging phase come from the flexion of the hip, the forward movement of the center of gravity, and the momentum of the leg. The heel strike announces the end of the walking cycle and the supporting phase begins again.

These two phases overlap for about twenty-five percent of the walking cycle, during the time when the body weight has moved on to the supporting leg and the other leg touches the ground. In a complete cycle one leg is involved in the supporting phase for sixty percent of the cycle and in the swinging phase for forty percent of the time. The faster the walk, the less the percentage of overlap.

It is this overlapping factor that distinguishes walking from other modes of locomotion. In

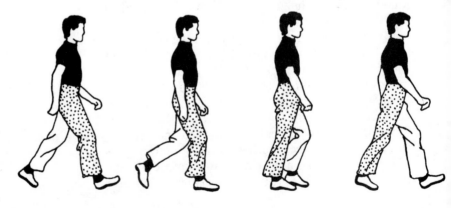

running, hopping, and jumping there are periods of levitation, when both feet are completely off the ground. In walking there is always at least one foot in contact with the ground.

Rotations during the cycle

During the course of one walking cycle there is a complex pattern of rotations at the hip, knee, and ankle. The rotations at these three joints are constantly shifting, but seldom in the same direction simultaneously. The net effect is that in the entire cycle the lower limb as a whole reverses its direction no less than thirteen times.

The hip flexes and extends once per cycle. During the support phase, starting at the heel strike of the leg in question, the hip is continually extended as the trunk moves forward over the supporting leg. After the other leg provides some support, the hip flexes and remains flexed during the swing phase. These activities are conducted by means of the femur about the pelvis.

The knee flexes and extends twice during the walking cycle. At the beginning of the support phase the knee has started a slow flexion which is maintained as the trunk moves forward over the supporting leg. As the body passes over the leg the knee extends obliquely backwards. Then, as the swing phase begins, the knee is rapidly flexed so that the foot can clear the ground while the leg swings forward. At the end of the swing phase the knee extends rapidly just before the next heel strike, thus

A complete walking cycle is from heel contact to the next heel contact of the same foot.

projecting the lower leg.

The ankle flexes and rotates twice per cycle. At the start of the support phase the ankle is flexed, which projects the heel forward. The ankle extends as the forefoot comes down to the ground after the heel strike. Once the whole of the foot is on the ground the ankle abruptly reverses from extension to flexion, reaching its maximum as the body passes over the supporting leg. After the body has passed the base of support, the ankle extends until the only contact with the ground is at the ball of the foot. Finally, the ankle quickly flexes again for the heel strike. All that activity in the lower limbs is matched and sometimes exceeded by the rest of a walking body. In particular the pelvis, thorax and arms rotate, gyrate, tilt, pivot, or swing.

The pelvis and thorax (the part between the neck and pelvis) twist in opposite horizontal directions, clockwise and counter-clockwise, during the walking cycle. The degree of these rotations, which produce a twisting and untwisting of the trunk, varies highly between individuals, and in the case of pelvic rotation, by the sex of the walker. Wider female pelvises are unable to move as far forward as the male versions. Therefore women walk with greater pelvic rotation, a phenomenon that does not go unnoticed by red-blooded male walkers and those females who would gain their attention. (From the age of seven or eight the girls of Papua, New Guinea, are taught the finer points of this vibrato technique and develop a more provocative walk which they can turn off and on at will.) While these horizontal rotations are going on the pelvis also tilts downward at an average of five degrees from the horizontal on the side of the swinging leg. This tilt is permitted by the bending of the knee during the swing phase. After the age of sixty-five these pelvic components of the walking step tend to be emphasized because in old age the muscle sense is slower and less accurate and the sense of balance in the inner ear is reduced. Thus an older person walks with a wider stance for more support, and shorter steps to help maintain equilibrium. However a lifetime of walking can help prevent the exaggerated widely-balanced stance and short-stepped stride of elderly walkers.

Arm swings, which are highly variable depending on speed and individual body style, are most commonly conducted across the body and not straight ahead. This action is made up of a forward rotation of the shoulder girdle on the side of the supporting leg and a flexion at the elbow of the arm above that leg.

The center of gravity

When a person walks they take their center of gravity on an undulating path as circuitous as a modified version of a roller coaster ride. This can be illustrated by means of a mythical experiment involving a walker with two pieces of chalk and a tunnel. The walker is equipped with a piece of chalk tied on top of the head and another tied on one hip at fifty-five percent of total body height. This latter location is the center of gravity while standing. The next step would be to find a tunnel exactly the height of the walker's head and walk down it while pressing the chalked hip to the wall and the head to the roof of the tunnel. One of the curiosities of walking is that a person is actually shorter when striding than standing. In fact the walker could stride down that tunnel with the certainty of one half inch of clearance. At the end of the tunnel journey the walker would have left a matching set of chalk lines describing two smooth, undulating curves that are almost exactly equal. These are the vertical and horizontal pathways of the displacements of gravity. Measurements would reveal that the curves of the chalk line on the top of the tunnel — the horizontal path of the center of gravity — would deviate from right to left approximately one and three quarter inches. The chalk line on the side wall of the tunnel — the vertical path of the center of gravity — would undulate up and down approximately one and four-fifths inches.

It is impossible for anyone to "walk the straight and narrow" but many of the movements of walking are geared to smoothing out the peaks and valleys of the center of gravity, which helps conserve energy. In order to produce an even, energy-efficient walk the

The tunnel test would show the almost equal paths of the center of gravity.

pelvis helps flatten the vertical pathway by rotating. The pelvic tilt lowers the center of gravity during the support phase and knee and foot mechanisms serve to smooth out any abrupt changes in the vertical pathway. The horizontal route of the center of gravity is kept down to its one and three quarter inches by the slight sideways motion of the legs in walking. This deviation from a precisely straight ahead direction minimizes the lateral displacement of the pelvis, thus flattening the horizontal pathway. Individual variations in walking are due to exaggerations of one or more of these gravity-stabilizing movements.

The walking muscles

Starting from a standstill, walking begins when the muscles of the calf relax and the body sways for-

134

ward, with gravity supplying the energy needed to overcome the walker's inertia. From that point on the action of many muscles takes place. The front thigh muscles contract for a fraction of a second, with a sort of rippling movement, to swing the leg forward. Simultaneously, muscles on the front of the lower leg contract to pull up the foot and prevent it from dragging just before the heel strikes.

As the heel strikes the ground, all the thigh and lower leg muscles must contract to stabilize the knee and ankle until the body weight is thrust forward by the calf muscles. Now the hip muscles swing the thigh forward, then stabilize it. This muscular activity is concentrated on the outer side of the thigh to prevent the pelvis from falling on the inner side as the weight goes on the leg.

While all of these lower limb muscles are thus engaged, those in the thorax or trunk must contract to hold the body erect and help swing the legs. The principal muscles involved here are located in the abdomen, sides, back, and chest. When the arm swings forward it does so by the contraction of the flexor muscles of the shoulder and forearm. On the return arm swings, muscles opposite these come into play.

To enable all of the walking muscles to work, others in the diaphragm, abdomen, and ribs expand the chest and lungs in the act of breathing. The only major muscles in the body that have not been used so far are those in the head and neck. But these, too, are used by walkers interested in their surroundings. Heads swivel on neck muscles and even those muscles which control the eyeballs are active during any walk worthy of the name. Finally, should a walker be in the company of others, jaw muscles will be given a workout during conversation.

CHAPTER ELEVEN

"A foot more light, a step more
true,
Ne'er from the heath-flower dashed
the dew;
Even the slight harebell raised its
head,
Elastic from her airy tread."
Walter Scott

11

How to Walk Better

A short course in the art and science of walking, and how to combine them to create style, grace, beauty, and pleasure.

The physical act of walking requires that inertia be overcome. Much of that inertia is mental. The first step in walking is to want to walk.

"Will moves through desire," as Aristotle said on one of his walks. If we are to follow in his admirable footsteps we must desire to overcome the apathy that keeps us stationary and is the major obstacle in a walker's way. Once this indifference is mastered, however, we are well on our way to experiencing the *Exhilarations of the Road,* as outlined by John Burroughs in his essay on that theme: "Persons who find themselves spent in a short walk to the market or the post office, or to do a little shopping, wonder how it is that their pedestrian friends can compass so many weary miles and not fall down from sheer exhaustion; ignorant of the fact that the walker is a kind of projectile that drops near or far according to the expansive force of the motive that set it in motion. In other words, the will or corporeal mainspring, whatever it be, is capable of being wound up to different degrees of tension."

Winding up one's corporeal mainspring to go walking is easy because walking is *fun!* It is one of the few forms of exercise that can be done with a smile. He who laughs, lasts. "Laughter is the shortest distance between two people" observed the comedi-

Plato was an advocate of lighthearted walking.

an, Victor Borge. It is also the shortest distance between two points. Aristotle, too, supported the idea of light-hearted walking when he declared laughter to be "a bodily exercise precious to health".

The philosophy of walking can be heavy going at times. "See that ye walk circumspectly, not as fools, but as wise," decrees Ephesians, Chapter 5, verse 15. Yet the fact remains that walking is child's play, and Plato said: "Life must be lived as play." Fun and frolic go hand in hand with walking. Unlike organized games with their strict boundaries and formal rules, walking allows for spontaneity. It is a game you can play to your heart's content as William Hazlitt related in his essay of 1822, entitled *On Going A Journey:* "Give me the clear blue sky over my head, and the green turf beneath my feet, a winding road before me and a three hours' march to dinner — and then to thinking! It is hard if I cannot start some game on these lone heaths. I laugh, I run, I leap, I sing for joy."

The standing start

"Why, then, do you walk as if you had swallowed a ramrod?" queried Epicetus in 60 A.D. Granted, the instructions for carriage found in Proverbs said: "A man of understanding walketh uprightly" and "He that walketh uprightly walketh surely", but Epicetus felt that the uprightly factor might have been overstressed. Not so the French Foreign Legion, where the proverbial ramrod theory of walking posture was desirable. To achieve this end a coin was placed between the buttocks of a raw recruit and he was ordered to march around without dropping the money.

Epicetus was right. The ramrod theory is wrong. Walking begins from a standing start and it is here that good walking posture begins. If the correct standing start is achieved, walking will be graceful, effortless, and strain on muscles and joints will be minimized. All of this can be accomplished without a coin or a ramrod.

Erect posture is a state of equilibrium maintained by means of reflexes. Standing askew disturbs the natural center of gravity and tenses a number of

140

muscles that are then forced to work abnormally in order to keep equilibrium. You can feel this for yourself by standing with your feet parallel and about a foot apart. Now swing your body slowly backward and forward like a pendulum from the ankle joints, while keeping heels and toes flat on the floor. You will feel the muscle tension at the extremes of each pendular swing. As you return to a vertical position the tension relaxes and then disappears at a certain point. This is your proper standing position but it is not exactly vertical. You can prove this by standing in front of a mirror and drawing imaginary plumb lines from your pelvic promontories to the floor. You will discover that most of your body weight is over the balls of your feet and not the heels. Prove it further by swinging back until your body weight is over your heels, and then forward again to the balance position over the balls of your feet. While over the heel position you will feel tension in your legs and back. To return to the balls of the feet brings relief.

Once you have got the hang of your proper standing position you can enhance it further by checking for your lumbar sway. When standing at ease, without tightening the muscles in your knees, pelvis, abdomen, or buttocks and without consciously gripping the ground with your toes, you will be able to detect a slight sway as your body quietly does battle with gravity to maintain your state of equilibrium. You should feel as if you are resting in time with the sway. Now you can prepare the rest of your body for walking. Elevate your chest a fraction and let your shoulders fall naturally to the sides. Your arms will follow suit and hang free and loose. Check your head and neck for flexibility by turning your head slightly without moving your neck. Bring your head into line by imagining that, like a marionette, it is on a string attached to the hindmost part of your crown.

Imaginary plumb lines from pelvic promontories reveal secrets of weight distribution.

No strings attached

In order to manipulate your wooden body, a puppeteer would control your actions with a major string, attached to your center of gravity, with which to propel your torso. The pendular limbs would follow mechanically with the help of supplementary strings on your head, shoulders, elbows, fingers, knees, ankles, heels, and toes. Then you would walk — like a puppet. Without a brain to coordinate limbs and muscles, movements would be jerky and unnatural.

Because walking is a reflex action, focusing undue attention on any part of the gait can develop tensions that disturb natural rhythm and coordination. A parable about a centipede, the champion of insect walkers, illustrates this possibility. The multi-legged creature was asked which set of legs he used to start walking. This question took the member of the order of *Chilopoda* by surprise and when he began to ponder it he found he could hardly move. What had formerly been a perfectly natural means of progression now became an immobilizing problem.

In order to avoid the experience of the centipede and to be able to walk with no strings attached, one might well heed the warning of an old Turkish proverb which says: "Before you love, learn to walk through the snow leaving no footprints." The mechanics of good walking should first be mastered and incorporated into the stride and then mentally set aside so that you can enjoy unencumbered all the pleasures afoot. Unless you suffer from physical abnormalities, the ingredients of good walking are already at your feet. All you have to do is dust them off, then mix them together to turn out a fine walk. If you have been walking incorrectly it may take a little effort and time to right the habit; it is unlikely to take very long. Most people who walk badly do so simply because they have never thought about it.

Efficient walking

The original point of walking was to cover long distances economically. Fossil remains, nearly two million years old, show that early man had already developed the structure necessary for a smooth, energy-conserving, striding gait. An efficient walk will maximize energy storage in the muscular system and minimize energy loss through ungainly movements. As well, it will prevent strain and fatigue and make walking as effortless as it was intended to be.

Proper alignment of the limbs permits the full flexibility of the joints, thereby reducing the amount of energy required in walking. When walking knock-kneed, the knees interfere with the natural pendular motion of the legs, necessitating a wider lateral stance which can lead to a duck-walk. This curious stride, while acceptable in a duck, in the human species causes the body to sway too far from side to side as the center of gravity shifts to and fro over feet that are too widely spaced. Fat thighs inhibit walking in a similar way by forcing a wider stance and causing a duck-waddle. Occasionally this motion can be useful, as in the sailor's nautical roll which helps maintain stability. In a normal gait, however, the feet should be placed no more than two or three inches apart — just far enough to prevent the knees from knocking together. This brings the center of gravity directly over each supporting foot and reduces the work of walking. Too much toe-in or toe-out is inefficient because it reduces the propulsive force of walking to either side, instead of straight ahead. Toes that point inward are sometimes misleadingly referred to as pigeon toes — a condition that tends to hinder flight. A certain amount of toe-out is necessary for lateral stability but it should not measure more than about fifteen degrees, which is normal. Anything more extreme leads to a flat-footed gait which places unnecessary strain on the ligaments in the inner knees and feet. One curious fact is that people who walk with excessive toe-out tend to stand with their hands turned out. Skiing is a useful exercise to correct wayward toes. In walking proper alignment can be achieved by facing your kneecaps directly forward. This lines up the knees and ankles and permits your joints to flex easily. Because your ankles are at a slightly oblique angle, your feet will turn outward as they should when your knees face forward.

The fashion model's walk, placing one foot directly in front of the other, is a waste of time and energy. Its effect is to emphasize the pelvic sway, which is already more pronounced in women than in men because of the greater female pelvic width. It

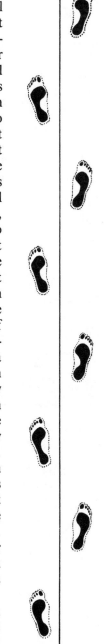

The footprints of an efficient walker.

143

also restricts shoulder movement, while wildly undulating hips and excessive pelvic rotation cause an inefficient, weaving walk. It looks much better than it walks. Tight-rope walkers use it, but it isn't necessary on terra firma.

An inspection of your footprints can show up any pigeon, duck, or tight-rope walking tendencies that you may have. Walk through snow or sand, or with wet feet across the bathroom floor, then draw a straight line between your footprints. Ideally you should see a set of parallel prints with toes that point just slightly outward (fifteen degrees from the straight line) and heels that come to within two or three inches of the line. Your steps should not cross over it as in pigeon-toed walking or tread directly along it as if it were a tight-rope.

Your foot should perform like a rocking chair with every step it takes. In this way the weight of your body never bears down for more than an instant on any part of the foot and is distributed in a rocking manner which aids momentum. At the beginning of each footfall your weight is borne by the heel which quickly transfers it along the outside border of the foot, across the forefoot to the big toe, which gives a final thrust as it leaves the ground. This motion helps minimize foot strain and fatigue and cushions shocks.

Slippery surfaces such as ice and wet grass reduce ground friction and hinder walking, while sand, snow, and other soft surfaces underfoot require a greater horizontal thrust to maintain the desired propulsive effect. Walking in these conditions is better accomplished with shorter, stronger steps than usual.

A jaunty, bouncing walk, although associated with high spirits, is inefficient because it wastes energy in exerting an upward force that exceeds the force of gravity. This results from placing the body weight too far back over the propelling leg by holding the trunk vertical, or even backward. Instead of taking off with the toes and pushing the body forward with the assistance of gravity, the propelling leg must fight against gravity. To prevent this all walking requires a slight forward lean, more so at higher speeds. The forward lean is accomplished most efficiently when the body weight is shifted from the ankles rather than the hips. Shifting from the hips also puts added strain on the lower back as well as being a poor place from which to move the center of gravity forward.

Walking uphill requires a greater forward lean to keep the center of gravity over the feet and make it easier to apply the force necessary to move it in a forward direction. (The reverse applies in a downhill walk when a slight backward lean is best.) To help develop your forward leaning posture, you can walk with a weighted pack on your back or with your hands clasped behind you. On a windy day a walker must lean further forward than usual, adjusting to gusts to maintain balance.

When you walk with your hands in your pockets you can quickly see how the restriction of the free swing of the arms is transferred to the pelvis and influences your walk. The movements of the lower limbs and the pelvic swing in walking are counterbalanced by the swinging of the arms. It is the rotating movement of the shoulders that makes the arms swing. The arms don't use any force to swing; on the contrary it takes muscular force to prevent them from doing so. If the arms are swung too vigorously an inefficient rotation of the upper body is introduced. Arms should be swung in time with the legs so that in fast walking the arm action can be exaggerated to help move the trunk forward.

When walking, all the major weight masses of the body — the head, trunk, and pelvis — should be kept in line. This facilitates balance, lessens fatigue, and prevents postural strain. Protruding posteriors and heads that are too far forward stand in the way of efficient walking. Your head, which weighs twelve or thirteen pounds, should be balanced over your spine so that it is perpendicular to a point midway through your hips — your center of gravity.

Tension is one of the enemies of an easy stride. Since many people in Western civilizations suffer from chronic muscular tension in the hips, buttocks, back, and abdomen, these tensions obstruct the free development of walking movements. The legs cannot swing loosely from the hips, but are carried stiffly and inharmoniously forward. Slippery floors can also be a cause of rigidity in walking. Our reflexes tell us to tighten our muscles in order not to lose our footing and we become accustomed to walking that way. A pair of rubber-soled shoes can eliminate this.

Go not like a ninny

In 1663 Francis Hawkins laid down his commandments for proper walking in a tome entitled *Youths Behaviour*.

> Go not like a ninny.
> Move not to and fro in walking.
> Hang not thy hands downwards.
> Shake not thine arms.
> Kick not the earth with thy feet.
> Throw not thy legs across, here and there.
> Trail not thy feet after thee.
> Truss not up thy breeches at every hand.
> Go not in a tripping manner with thy heels.
> Go not upon the top of thy toes.
> Go not in a dancing fashion.
> Thou shalt not stoop.
> Thou shalt not caper.

It is not surprising that there is a bit of a ninny in many of us. The feat of walking is no mean task. For every single step we take, thirty different muscles must be started, accelerated, decelerated, and stopped. Operating from a constantly shifting base that at times is no larger than a coin, we have to balance the teetering structure of our body — an act not unlike a juggler balancing a six foot pole on his chin. Small wonder that we sometimes caper and throw our legs across, here and there. Though quaint and dated, Hawkins' instructions for proper walking contain several truths.

To avoid walking like a ninny, Hawkins' list can be supplemented with points outlined earlier in this chapter:

> Keep thy head and upper body in line.
> Thou shalt lean slightly forward.
> Let thine arms swing freely.
> Thy knees shall face forward.

"Thou shalt not walk like a ninny."

146

Keep thy feet two or three inches apart.
Thy toes shall face slightly outward.
Thou shalt rock from heel to toe.
Go forth not tense, but relaxed.

One of the easiest ways of practicing this preaching is to walk for a while with a longer stride than usual. This serves to accentuate your present style and expose any faults. A lengthened stride also allows your locomotive mechanism to perform more freely by shaking up its various elements so that they fall naturally into place.

Rhythm

"Hup, two, three, four; hup, two, three, four," bellows the drill sergeant to his troops, in an effort to drum some rhythm into their step by calling out a cadence. Plato said: "Man's life stands in need of good rhythm." And so does his stride. Rhythm and harmony are fundamental elements in the symphony of good walking. Musical accompaniment, sung or unsung, can help tune our bodies into a harmonious walk. Barking drill sergeants, marching music, work songs, and sea shanties establish an easy, if sometimes vigorous, flowing rhythm for walking. Scottish reels and Irish jigs liven up the tempo when there is a need to get going. But the works of Mozart and those whose "music has charms to soothe a savage breast" can be walked to so that "rhythm and harmony find their way into the inmost places of the soul, imparting grace and making the soul of him who is rightly musical, graceful" (Plato).

Of course, it is not necessary to have a soaring symphony swirling around in your head or even to hum the lyrics of an up-tempo ditty. Just try to walk with a smooth, flowing grace and with all the components of your body in harmony. And one of the simplest ways to begin to walk with rhythm in your sole is to begin by lengthening your stride.

Step and stride

Each of us has a personal stride at which we walk most comfortably and fall into quite unconsciously. In a short work entitled *Walking Tours,* Robert Louis Stevenson discussed his personal preference:

"I do not approve of leaping and running. Both of these hurry the respiration; they both shake up the brain out of its glorious open-air confusion; and they break the pace. Uneven walking is not so agreeable to the body, and it distracts and irritates the mind. Whereas, once you have fallen into an equable stride, it requires no conscious thought from you to keep it up."

There are several things you can do to find your "equable stride", the easiest of which is to try lengthening your present one. Many of us walk with steps that are too short. Most of the energy in walking is consumed by the motions of your center of gravity. Short steps make it harder to push it around and force your body into abrupt movements that expend more energy. Longer strides take the weight off your feet by smoothing out the path of your center of gravity and creating momentum that pushes it forward with less effort. This enables you to walk faster and keep up your pace longer because, in efficient walking, you actually store up energy in your muscular system.

You can check to see how your present stride measures up with others. One full stride is composed of two step lengths. (One step from one leg gets you half way and another step from the other leg completes the stride.) Studies of average stride lengths show that in normal walking yours will measure about eighty-nine percent of your height and in fast walking, one hundred and six percent of your height. If you are five feet six inches in height, your stride length will be about fifty-nine inches. When you accelerate, stride length will increase to almost seventy inches, four more than your body height.

The step length, half a stride, is the distance measured from heel to heel of the same foot from where it takes off to where it touches the ground. The shortest possible step length has been pegged at about thirteen inches — anything less than that and you are shuffling. The step length of the French army is set at almost thirty inches, and at nearly thirty-two inches in the German army. The non-military step of an average person is about twenty-

Soldiers march with a precisely measured step length.

four inches in length.

Somewhere within your present short, choppy stride there quite likely hides a longer, smoother, more rhythmical one. Free it from the physical bonds of tight clothing and bad footwear, or the psychological fetters of tension, and watch how your walk improves.

Speed

The discovery of your personal stride will pave the way for speed. Robert Louis Stevenson's condemnation of "leaping and running" echoed Shakespeare's words from *Romeo and Juliet:* "Wisely and slow; they stumble that run fast." Some latter day philosophers like Alvin Toffler feel that speed may be one of the enemies of mankind. In his book, *Future Shock,* he shows how we experience "dizzying disorientation brought on by the premature arrival of the future". Nowadays we have easy access to speed provided by artificial means of locomotion. Airplanes toy with the speed of sound, cars propel us along motorways at, and often beyond, speed limits set by anxious governments. Crack express trains often exceed one hundred miles per hour. When the first steam locomotive hit the track in 1825 it managed a then staggering thirteen miles per hour. Prior to that one could travel only as fast as a horse. In 1688 in *Holmes Armoury,* published in England, it was stated that "Walk is the sloest pace a Horse doth go; it is used to cool a Horse after hard Riding." In 1832 a British army instruction manual decreed that the rate of marching was not to exceed four miles an hour.

The speed of walking is the product of step length multiplied by the number of steps taken in a given period of time. The French army marches at a pace of one hundred and twenty-eight steps per minute, the German army one hundred and fourteen, and the United States army at an average brisk walking pace composed of one hundred and six steps each minute.

Armies march with a precisely measured step so that everyone is taking the prescribed number of steps per minute. The rest of us are not so orderly. The number of steps per minute to reach certain walking speeds will vary according to height.

On a treadmill a walker measuring five feet eight inches in height took one hundred, one hundred and twelve, one hundred and twenty-two, and one hundred and thirty steps per minute to achieve speeds of two and a half, three, three and a half, and four miles per hour, respectively. To reach those same speeds a six foot walker took ninety-two, one hundred, one hundred and five, and one hundred and eight steps per minute.

The generally accepted average walking speed is about three miles per hour over level ground. Up hill and down dale efforts reduce the average to two and a half miles per hour. Most people can maintain this pace without undue exertion for an extended period of time. The current record for a non-stop walk is just over three hundred miles at an average speed of about two and a half miles per hour. (Race walking, with exaggerated arm pumping and a swivel hipped action plus locked knees, is much faster than normal walking. A race walker can maintain a speed of eight miles an hour for ten miles, which is faster than many people can jog.) A brisk walk may cover more ground in a given time and the effort may be more rigorous, creating greater circulatory and respiratory involvement than a slow run or jog.

When you want to walk faster you simply increase your stride length and speed up your leg swings, which reduces the length of time in contact with the ground. Almost anyone can exceed their normal walking speed by about forty percent. This gives an average brisk speed over level ground of about four miles per hour. Less fit people should work up to their brisk speed over a period of time.

Walking speed is a personal thing between yourself and the blue sky overhead; if you are doing it for exercise there is no need to work yourself up into a lather. The American Medical Association publication, *Today's Health,* has said that physical fitness depends on how much we exercise our muscles, not our sweat glands. An ancient Spanish proverb summed it up: "Walk till the blood appears on the cheek, not the sweat on the brow."

Distance

Once we begin playing around with stride and speed, we inevitably arrive at distance. A mile is five thousand, two hundred and eighty feet as the crow flies. But if a person walks at two feet per step, a mile is two thousand, six hundred and forty steps. If you were to count each of those steps, your mile would seem a great deal further than that. Fortunately there are so many other distractions during most walks that we are seldom reduced to numbering our steps. The miles sneak by without our noticing it. At first to walk a mile might sound like a major trek; when translated into time, a twenty minute walk is less of an obstacle. Most of us achieve at least twenty minutes walking a day. At three miles per hour that is a magic mile.

In Switzerland and other alpine countries in Europe where walking rules, routes are signposted with average walking times as well as metric distance. Walkers experienced in the ups and downs of mountains have a rule of thumb, or foot, concerning heights. The British call it Naismith's Rule: "Estimate an hour for every three miles off the map plus one hour for every two thousand feet (six hundred and fifty meters)." Whether up or downhill, you should allow another hour for an altitude change of two thousand feet. This rule applies to an unladen walker. Packs add more time.

Another way of disguising or making light of distance is to walk in sections by landmarks. In Switzerland for instance, most footpaths have signs at regular intervals that keep you informed as to your distance from the nearest wine and cheese. This kind of landmark serves to inspire a walker as do the closeup Ordnance Survey maps of Britain which show the location of all the pubs. In city walking you can measure your miles by streets. Most North American cities are laid out on a grid system which equals about twenty city blocks to the mile.

Boredom can be more of a factor in city walking. When you walk from A to B to A, it is easy to overlook the fact that one half of your walk will be taken up with your return journey. You might want to vary your route; in fact, the longer way round may well be the shorter way home. Other tricks to make the miles fly by are seeking out the shady side of the street on a hot day, or the sheltered side when the wind is harsh. Variety, in the form of city parks with grass underfoot instead of concrete is the spice of a city walker's life.

You should plan rest stops for any walks over an hour's duration. The old marching British army halted for ten minutes every hour for a drink and a rest. No other halts were permitted. With kits weighing in at forty-eight pounds, they covered four miles every fifty minutes, and they did it for hours on end.

Long distance walkers have left several records for modern day competitive comparison. Captain Barclay Allardice walked 1000 miles in 1000 hours to collect a wager of 1000 guineas. This feat, achieved in England in 1809, left him none the worse for wear, although he lost twenty pounds in weight en route. Another walker hot-footed it across Asia covering 6800 miles in 238 days.

Breathing

Whatever the distance, you will need to breathe. Like walking, it is such a natural accomplishment that most of us tend to take it for granted. Again, like walking, many of us do not do it properly. Nevertheless, the action of the lungs is one of the most important links in the chain of events unleashed by the act of walking.

At rest we use no more than one tenth of total lung capacity. The enormity of this neglect can be appreciated if it is realized that the three hundred million tiny air sacs called *alveoli* form a lung surface area forty times greater than that of the entire body. With the aid of a network of slender capillaries, the *alveoli* transfer oxygen into the red blood corpuscles which then carry it throughout the body to nourish every cell. At the same time these air sacs take used carbon dioxide from the corpuscles and send it outside with each breath. Proper breathing promotes the oxygenation of the blood and the elimination of waste carbon dioxide.

There may be other benefits obtainable from the

152

air in which we move, as Dr. Donald Norfolk has observed in *The Habits of Health. Spiritus,* a Latin word denoting both "breath" and "life force", is the root of the words "spirit" and "inspiration". Even before oxygen was known to exist, the yogis of India sought to gain control of *prana,* a vital force they believed to be extracted from the air in breathing and to bring health and vitality to every organ. A classical Sanskrit text, *Shiva Sanhita,* points out that one who breathes properly "becomes healthy and likeable and emits a pleasant odor, and there will be good appetite and digestion, cheerfulness, a good figure, courage and enthusiasm and strength."

The earth is surrounded by five quadrillion tons of air which at sea level exert a pressure of 14.73 pounds per square inch. If you are of average size, this means that your surface area of twenty square feet must walk through a continual pressure of nearly nineteen tons of air. All that heavy air represents another kind of pressure on your lungs. Depending on where you live, you will inhale up to twenty billion particles of foreign matter a day. For this reason you should breathe through your nose, which traps most of that pollution in the mucous lining the nasal passages. Breathing through the nose, as opposed to the mouth, also helps to warm the air to body temperature before it reaches the lungs.

The key to proper breathing is to do it deeply and in a relaxed manner. Concentrate on inhaling until your lungs are filled to capacity, then exhaling to expel every ounce of air. Develop a breathing rhythm by inhaling steadily for three or four steps, then exhaling for the next three or four steps. Regular practice of this exercise will improve lung capacity and soon you will find that you can take more steps with each breath. Don't overdo it; over-breathing can make some people dizzy. Mrs. Ella Wheeler Wilcox, an American poet and journalist who lived around the turn of the century, recommended that words suggesting vitality and life be repeated when breathing in, and words evoking thoughts of rest and relaxation be mouthed when breathing out. For example, you might mentally recite something like:

Awake ... Awake ... Awake ... Awake with your breathing-in steps. For your breathing-out steps you could try: Asleep ... Asleep ... Asleep ... Asleep. Substitute any words of your choice — walking will give you the inspiration — and you will find your breathing/thinking/walking routine will benefit your lungs/mind/body.

Once mastered, good breathing habits can be forgotten and nature allowed to take its course. Your body breathes best when it is walking. The upright posture puts all of the breathing apparatus into its proper position; the physical demands of walking stimulate the lungs into action.

CHAPTER TWELVE

"Whose furthest footstep never
strayed
Beyond the village of his birth
Is but a lodger for the night
In this old wayside inn of earth."
Richard Hovey

12

The World at Our Feet

The remarkable foot-to-mind syndrome, the psychological and spiritual benefits of walking, and some inspiration for walkers.

In the beginning, it was the ability to walk that led to the development of the new and improved version of the ape that eventually became *homo sapiens* — knowing man. There is strong evidence that a return to the basic act of walking would continue the

Words of wisdom from walkers like Shakespeare are inspirational.

process of evolution and spur humanity on to yet greater feats.

If walking created our minds in the first place, then it should be able to expand them further. Walking can be a source of inspiration and creativity for an inventive mind. It stimulates the thought processes into action and provides answers for an inquiring mind. But it can also tranquilize a troubled mind. It can be an avenue of discovery for a lost soul or a path of escape for an unsettled one.

Walking is a key of life that can unlock secrets of ourselves. It is a tonic for flagging spirits and an elixir for a deflated ego. It is a road to an enriched spirit that leads to increased self-respect. Walking is a lost escape route to freedom and pleasure waiting to be rediscovered by the twentieth century.

Some of the greatest minds of all time have set examples for us to follow. Many great men of letters who were enthusiastic walkers have left us legacies.

He hath left you all his walks, ·
His private arbours, and new-planted
orchards, — common pleasures,
To walk abroad, and recreate yourselves.

(William Shakespeare)

Awareness

Movement is the basis of awareness. We cannot sense, feel, or think without movement. Our every action, mental as well as physical, originates with muscular activity. Our behavior is governed by a complex of mobilized muscles, senses, feelings, and thoughts. The part of the brain that makes us walk, the motor cortex, lies only a few millimeters away from the part of the brain strata that deals with the association process, thought, and feeling. The proximity of the two means that walking, which mobilizes the motor cortex, has a parallel effect on thinking and feeling.

In the waking state we experience sensatio through the traditional five senses plus a kinestheti sense related to, and dependent on movement whicl tells us of pain or pleasure and makes us aware of oui orientation in space and the passage of time. When we are moving and thus aware, we have feelings of joy, grief, anger, self-respect or lack of it, and other conscious and unconscious emotions. When we are aware we can think through the functions of the intellect and know the opposites of right and left, good and bad, right and wrong. We can understand, know, classify, and remember. All of these processes are first activated, then stimulated by movements of muscles. These include all changes in the temporal states of the body: breathing, eating, speaking, blood circulation, digestion, and so on.

An old Tibetan parable uses an analogy between a horse and carriage to explain how this works. The muscles are a team of horses. Behind them is a carriage which is the skeleton of a man. Riding in the carriage are desires. The coachman is the state of awareness. When the coachman is unmoved and thus unaware, the carriage is dragged about aimlessly as the horses pull in different directions. Each passenger wants off at a different destination, but is unable to do so because the carriage will not stop. When the coachman is moving and aware, he holds the reins properly and controls the horses so that every passenger gets where he wants to go.

The natural world was meant to be walked through.

The act of walking creates a state of awareness so that we are at one with our body. Our carriage is on the right road so that we can perceive, comprehend, make discoveries, invent, create, innovate, and know.

Walking is the speed at which we were designed to comprehend our surroundings. When we walk through life at three miles per hour we experience it to the hilt. We can explore it, feel it, and respond to it. When we move too fast, life becomes a blur. But speed has always attracted us. In her book, *Wandering,* Ruth Rudner describes the lure of speed: "High speeds are alluring even to those who fear them. Wheels spin faster than the world, and one is sucked willingly into the vortex of a whirlwind, any whirlwind. Beguiled and seduced by the sheer energy of the machine, one is in the end only spun up and flung out again. And flung out against what? Some, by now quite boring, existential void. I prefer to go for a walk." And she does, through the mountains of Europe where she experiences all: "I feel every raindrop, every thirst, hunger, ray of sun, every step I take. I feel the mountains and the earth. I am aware at every instant of my body. My mind senses all things through my body — feels, sees, smells, touches, understands with my body."

Walking helps slow down the treadmill which otherwise might spirit us off into oblivion. It limits us to a manageable speed that our senses and psyches can cope with. When we walk we are masters of our own destiny. Moving independently without timetables or schedules and without mechanical assistance increases our self-respect and sense of worth. Footpower, as opposed to horsepower, uplifts our spirits and increases our awareness of personal liberty. To move ourselves, rather than being enslaved by machines that shunt us about like commodities on a conveyor belt, restores our humanity.

Artificial environments tend to create artificial people. We have need of the sky. We need contact with the grass and we grow taller from walking with the trees. Technology insulates us from life but walking gets us back to basics and exposes us to our roots. When the currents of the universe can play through our bodies, our disguises fall away, our sympathies come to the fore, and the pores of our soul are opened wide. John Burroughs gave some of the reasons why we need the good Mother Earth beneath our feet: "Man takes root at his feet, and at best he is no more than a potted plant in his house or carriage till he has established communication with the soil by the loving and magnetic touch of his soles to it. Then the tie of association is born; then spring those invisible fibers and the rootlets through which character comes to smack of the soil, and which make a man kindred to the spot of earth he inhabits."

In an impassioned plea to get everyone to walk, Thomas Coryat (the "Odcombian Legge-stretcher" who wrote *Coryat's Crudities* in 1611) tended to rant and rave somewhat. But his comments, in old English, "to animate the learned to travel into the outlandish regions" remain valid today. He pointed out that "storkes, swallows and all the birds in the ayre, the wilde beasts in the woodes and forrests, the fishes and sea-monsters in the waters" and even "the starres in the celestiall skye" all move continuously.

Coryat's Odcombe-to-Venice shoes hung in his parish church for over a century.

"Therefore," quoth Coryat, "Goe forth whatsoever thou art that desires to maintaine, and retaine the dignity of thy nature, go forth I say, from these most miserable lurking holes, put off thy fetters, cast away that night from thy eyes, remove the mouldy rust and languishing faintnesse from thee, cast off thy drowsie disease, go forth of thy grave and sepulchre, wherein as if thou wert a man halfe dead, thou dost not enjoy the most pleasant sight and taste of natural things. Art thou in the earthe? and yet hast thou not seene the face of the earthe?"

Solvitur ambulando

The motto of "the philosophical tramp" — *solvitur ambulando* — is a Latin proverb which means: the matter, or the difficulty, is settled or solved by walking.

Walking helps solve all manner of matters and difficulties. It can also help us to avoid them in the

Many great minds took Thoreau's route to maintain mental equilibrium.

first place. As a means of escape it is unparalleled, if for no other reason than the fact that the walkers' way is usually less crowded. In *Confessions of an English Opium Eater,* Thomas De Quincey found that it is possible to walk away from a variety of problems: "I have generally found that, if you are in quest of some certain escape from Philistines of whatsoever class — sherrif-officers, bores, no matter what — the surest refuge is to be found amongst hedgerows and fields."

Walking helps banish cares and stamp out trials and tribulations. It is a mental purgative that washes the brain and flushes out the soul. Plato said that it "would almost cure a guilty conscience" and a medieval English adage saw walking as a cure-all:

From care, and cost and wisedomes folly,
He tooke his walke into a waie more holly.

Many of the great philosophers walked to think, but at least one of them denounced his profession in favor of walking as a means of psychological fitness.

Bertrand Russell wrote: "Unhappy businessmen would increase their happiness more by walking six miles a day than any conceivable change of philosophy." Russell walked and thought for over ninety years.

Walking has long been a panacea for the morbid tendencies of writers. Henry David Thoreau regarded his daily excursions around Walden Pond as essential for maintaining his mental equilibrium. "I think I cannot preserve my health and spirits unless I spend four hours a day at least — and it is commonly more than that — sauntering through the woods and over the hills and fields, absolutely free from all worldly engagements."

Even the greatest thinkers with the loftiest of ideals need to be brought back down to earth occasionally. Walking helps keep heads that are in the clouds in contact with reality. It clears overloaded minds and has contributed to the long and productive lives of many great humanitarians. Jeremy Bentham, the English Utilitarian philosopher, lived for eighty years after his birth in 1748. He wrote on ethics, jurisprudence, and political economy, and made valuable prison and poor law reforms. His walks helped him to arrive at his belief that the pursuit of the greatest happiness of the greatest number is the highest form of morality. His only self-indulgence took the form of regular "post-jentacular circumgyrations" afoot.

Rousseau had to walk before he could think.

Inspiration

"Never have I thought so much, never have I realized my own existence so much, been so much alive, been so much myself if I may say so, as in those journeys which I have made alone and on foot. Walking has something in it which animates and heightens my ideas: I can scarcely think when I stay in one place; my body must be set a-going if my mind is to work." Thus Jean Jacques Rousseau, the eighteenth century French philosopher, paid tribute to the role his feet played in developing his theory that men would be better and happier were they to return to a natural state.

Immanuel Kant, founder of the transcendental

school of philosophy, walked for one hour every afternoon. Later on, Friedrich Wilhelm Nietzsche, who walked and thought rather aggressively, took the idea of footpower several steps further. "A sedentary life is the real sin against the Holy Spirit. Only those thoughts that come by walking have any value."

Walking winds its way in and out of his theory of "superman" and his doctrine of the perfectibility of man through forcible self-assertion. For him, this road led to superiority over ordinary mortality. He used a precipitous footpath leading to the isolated hill village of Eze to help create his *Thus Spake Zarathustra.* He credited his toiling feet with taming, or at least helping out in the tussle with, his tempestuous thoughts. The footpath, Chemin Frederic Nietzsche, remains today. At its finish line near the gate to Eze, a plaque commemorating his feat reads in part: "... during the difficult ascent — the creative inspiration was strongest in me, when my muscles were working the hardest."

Whether or not Nietzsche's theories of supermen qualify for what John Steinbeck said in *The Grapes*

Wordsworth walked about 185,000 miles in his eighty years.

of Wrath is a matter of opinion. "Man, unlike any other thing organic or inorganic in the universe, grows beyond his work, walks up the stairs of his concepts, emerges ahead of his accomplishments." But there is no question that many illustrious walkers have built stairways of thought and left paths of glory which have enabled mankind to progress.

Aristotle started his Peripatetic school in 335 B.C. It was so named after his habit of walking up and down *(peripaton)* the paths of the Lyceum in Athens, while thinking or lecturing. His walking/thinking productions included works on zoology, physics, metaphysics, rhetoric (in the original sense of the word — the art of persuasive speaking or writing), and logic which he invented. He stopped walking only when he died in 322 B.C., the same year as Demosthenes who composed his famous orations while walking on a beach. Both of these gentlemen had studied under Plato who paced up and down in his outdoor schoolroom — an olive grove. Prior to Plato, Socrates had wandered around the streets of Athens in search of truth. Later the tradition of walking to learn was perpetuated in Rome by the *Ordo Vagorum,* the walking scholars.

When an admirer of Wordsworth's came to pay homage to him at his house in the English Lake District, he asked to see the study where the poetic wonders were wrought. A maid replied: "Here is his library, but his study is out of doors." Wordsworth is credited with averaging ten miles a day on his rounds in the Lakes and the Alps, and logging a grand total of some 185,000 miles during his eighty year lifetime. His romantic and lyrical poems frequently refer directly to the inspiration he encountered on his walks. At sixty he was credited with being as fit as he had been at twenty.

"Walking is the natural recreation for a man who desires not absolutely to suppress his intellect but to turn it out to play for a season," says Sir Leslie Stephen, the biographer, critic, historian of ideas, and father of Virginia Woolf. In his essay, *In Praise of Walking,* he continues: "All great men of letters have, therefore, been enthusiastic walkers (exceptions, of course, excepted)."

Certainly many of the British men of letters bear out his statement. The most lettered of them all, Shakespeare, conscientiously observed his own maxim: "Jog on, jog on, the footpath way." And his friend Ben Jonson walked from London to Scotland. Keats and Shelley walked mile upon mile. The author of *The Compleat Angler,* Isaak Walton, along with friends, began a day's fishing with a walk of twenty miles before they took "their morning draught". Most of the heroines of Jane Austen's novels were walkers, as was their creator. Presumably Jonathan Swift researched *Gulliver's Travels* during his daily ten mile hike. Another ten mile per day addict was Samuel Taylor Coleridge who produced *Kubla Khan* and *The Ancient Mariner,* and often walked through the Quantock Hills in south west England. The first stanzas of *The Ancient Mariner* were conceived on one of these walks. He was an addict of another kind, being a slave to opium as was De Quincey, but that did not prevent him from tallying forty miles in one day in Scotland. In the same country Sir Walter Scott, although he was lame, delighted in walks of twenty and thirty miles over the hills and crags of his native land.

Sydney Smith, the English churchman, essayist, and wit once said that "You shall never break down in a speech on the day on which you have walked twenty miles." When composing the talks that gave rise to his Methodism, the religious teacher, John Wesley, found that brisk walks of twenty and thirty miles a day put "spirit into his sermons". Dr. Samuel Johnson, made famous by his walking companion, Boswell, walked in spite of himself, according to Leslie Stephen: "Even the ponderous Johnson used to dissipate his early hypochondria by walking from Lichfield to Birmingham and back (thirty-two miles)."

Other aficionados of the "post-jentacular circumgyrations" enjoyed by Jeremy Bentham included the political economist, John Stuart Mill, and the writer on art and social subjects, John Ruskin. Up at six, walk six miles, then work six hours, was his formula. Scottish literary critic and

166

In terms of miles walked and words about it, Henry David Thoreau has few rivals.

historian, Thomas Carlyle, once managed a fifty-four mile walk in a day in the Highlands.

All of these people would have agreed with an observation of Ralph Waldo Emerson: "Walking has the best value as gymnastics of the mind." The American philosophic writer and essayist, who felt that "no pursuit has more breath of immortality in it" and wished that he had published a book called "The Art of Walking", helped establish a tradition of walking in America. (To treat a liver ailment he once walked a thousand miles in ninety days around his garden.) "Hurrah for what our fathers used to call shanks' mare", said the naturalist Joseph Wood Krutch, and Oliver Wendell Holmes, Nathaniel Hawthorne, John Muir, Theodore Roosevelt, John Burroughs, Edwin Way Teale, Lewis Mumford, Ray Bradbury, John James Audubon, and many others have walked and written about it. Like Walt Whitman, "afoot and light-hearted" they "took to the open road". But in terms of miles logged (probably as many as Wordsworth) and eloquence, Henry David Thoreau has few rivals.

Walking for art's sake is less well documented in languages other than English, but Basho — the greatest of all Japanese Haiku poets — walked for three years on a 1500 mile journey that resulted in his epic *Back Roads To Far Towns.* Johann Sebastian Bach, while a mere boy, once hiked two hundred miles to hear the renowned Buxtehude play the organ. As well as musical abilities, his illustrious sons also inherited his love of walking.

The story of creative walking is mainly an historical one. It may be a reflection of the current state of affairs in today's world that not many of those who shape our destinies rely on walking for inspiration. A return to the honorable tradition of thinking afoot might produce quite different ideas from those that are the product of people sitting behind desks. Henry Wadsworth Longfellow gave us food for thought:

Lives of great men all remind us
We can make our lives sublime,
And, departing, leave behind us
Footprints on the sands of time.

Where

Those of us not in a position to change the course of history, or not gifted with the ability to create works of art, can still enjoy the most profound walking benefit. The sheer pleasure of walking is available to all. We can walk anywhere in any landscape. Rupert Brooke wrote of the experience of landscapes that brought on such bliss that: "Breathless, we flung us on the windy hill, laughed in the sun and kissed the grass." Though we may be unable to express ourselves so passionately, the most insensitive of souls cannot help but respond favorably to the birds, bees, and flowers of a country walk. Even city walks, with people to watch and architecture to observe, can be good for the soul. The location matters not so much as the state of the spirit, which a walk anywhere will soon massage and soothe into a receptive and perceptive mood.

The French writer, Henri-Frédéric Amiel, kept a

walking diary. "1st February 1854. A walk. The atmosphere incredibly pure — a warm, caressing gentleness in the sunshine — joy in one's whole being ... I became young again, wondering, and simple, as candour and ignorance are simple. I abandoned myself to life and to nature, and they cradled me with a gentleness. To open one's heart in purity to this ever-pure nature, to allow this immortal life of things to penetrate into one's soul, is at the same time to listen to the voice of God. Sensation may be a prayer, and self-abandonment an act of devotion."

It is the intimacy of walking that leads to depths of experience like those of Amiel and enables a walker's universe to unfold as it should. Nothing opens doors for a mind, or educates an eye, as well as the practice of measuring a landscape by one's own legs.

Wandering through Switzerland, journeying through Britain, on foot in America — walking anywhere on the face of the earth can be a beautiful experience. In *A Fluvial Walk,* Thoreau waxed poetic about a barefoot trip he made down the middle of a trout stream, perhaps recalling a verse from *Cheerful Ayres For Three Voices,* by a medieval English poet named Wilson.

Do not fear to put thy feet
Naked in the river sweet
Think not that newt, nor leech, nor toad
Would bite thy foot where thou wouldst trode.

However, walking off the beaten track can sometimes test the spirit as Nathaniel Hawthorne described in his *American Notebook:* "Always when I flounder into the midst of a tract of bushes, which cross and intertwine themselves about my legs, and brush my face, and seize hold of my clothes with a multitudinous grip — always, in such a difficulty, I feel as it were almost as well to lie down and die in rage and despair, as to go one step further." But he recovered from such experiences to once again plunge "into a cool bath of solitude".

"Do not fear to put thy feet naked in the river sweet."

Walking is the most democratic of pastimes, so it is only fair to let the English essayist and caricaturist Max Beerbohm speak his piece. In fact he denounced it as a waste of time and energy in a short item — *Going Out For a Walk.* "It is a fact that not

"Every walk is a crusade to reconquer the Holy Land from the Infidels."

once in my life have I gone out for a walk. I have been taken out for walks; but that is another matter ... People seem to think there is something inherently noble and virtuous in the desire to go for a walk ... But, pending a time when no people wish me to go and see them, and I have no wish to go and see any one, and there is nothing whatever for me to do off my own premises, I will never go out for a walk."

In our mechanized times, many people regard pedestrians with feelings similar to those encountered by a German pastor named Carl Moritz who spent six weeks walking through England in 1782. He found that, to the Britons of that time, a walker was "considered as a sort of wild man or an out-of-the-way being who is stared at, pitied, suspected and shunned by everybody who meets him ... in England any person undertaking so long a journey on foot is sure to be looked upon and considered as either a beggar, or a vagabond, or some necessitous wretch, which is a character not more popular than a rogue. To what various, singular and unaccountable fatalities and adventures are not foot-travellers exposed in this land of carriages and horses?"

170

As if in response to the non-walkers of the world, Thoreau penned the following: "Every walk is a sort of crusade, preached by some Peter the Hermit in us, to go forth and reconquer this Holy Land from the hands of the Infidels."

"Walk and be happy; walk and be healthy" said Dickens.

When

A final inspirational thought from Charles John Huffam Dickens: "The sum of the whole is this; walk and be happy; walk and be healthy. The best way to lengthen our days is to walk steadily and with a purpose. The wandering man knows of certain ancients, far gone in years, who have staved off infirmities and dissolution by earnest walking — hale fellows, close upon ninety, but brisk as boys."

The best time to walk is now. Like Shakespeare, we should "make haste; the better foot before". Whether we walk around the block or around the world, a maxim from *Tao Te Ching* still applies: "The longest journey starts with just one step."

FOOTPRINTS

"Walk aside with me. I have studied eight or nine wise words to speak to you."
William Shakespeare

Footprints

Sources of information and further reading.

The author gratefully acknowledges reference to, and occasionally use of, material from the following sources:

American College of Sports Medicine: *Guidelines for Graded Exercise Testing and Exercise Prescription* — Lea and Febiger, Philadelphia (1975)

American College of Sports Medicine: "The Recommended Quantity and Quality of Exercise for Developing and Maintaining Fitness in Healthy Adults" — *Sports Medicine Bulletin* (July 1978)

Astrand, P.O. and Rodahl, K.: *Textbook of Work Physiology* — McGraw-Hill, New York (1970)

Belloc, Hilaire: *The Path to Rome* — Thomas Nelson & Sons, London and New York (1902)

Benedict, F.G. and Murschhauser, H.: *Energy Transformation During Horizontal Walking* — Carnegie Institute of Washington (1915)

Boothroyd, A.E.: *Fascinating Walking Sticks* — Salix Books, Bracknell, U.K. (1970)

Broer, M.R.: *Efficiency of Human Movement* — W.B. Saunders Company (1973)

Chapman, C.B. and Mitchell, J.H.: "The Physiology of Exercise" — *Scientific American* (May 1965)

Clarke, H.H.: "Physical Fitness" — *Research Digest* (January 1977)

Coryat, Thomas: *Coryat's Crudities* — James MacLehose and Sons, Glasgow (1903 — originally published in 1611)

Ducroquet, R.J.: *Walking and Limping* — J.B. Lippincott and Company, Philadelphia and Toronto (1968)

Durnin, J., Brockway, J., and Whitcher, H.: "Effects of a Short Period of Training of Varying Severity on Some Measurements of Physical Fitness" — *Journal of Applied Physiology* (1960)

Falls, H.B. and Humphrey, L.D.: "Energy Cost of Locomotion in Women" — *Medicine and Science in Sports* (1976)

Feldenkrais, M.: *Awareness Through Movement* — Harper and Row Publishing, New York (1972)

Fisher, S. and Gullickson, G.: *Energy Cost of Ambulation in Health and Disability* — Archive of Physical Medicine and Rehabilitation (1978)

Fletcher, Colin: *The Complete Walker* — Alfred A. Knopf Ltd. (1968)

Fruin, John J.: *Pedestrian Planning and Design* — Metropolitan Association of Urban Designers and Environmental Planners, Inc., New York (1971)

Gayle, R., Montoye, H. and Philpot, J.: "Accuracy of Pedometers for Measuring Distance Walked" — *Research Quarterly* (1977)

Gehlsen, G. and Dill, D.: "Comparative Performance of Men and Women in Grade Walking" — *Human Biology* (September 1977)

Graham, Stephen: *The Gentle Art of Tramping* — Robert Holden & Co. Ltd., London (1927)

Gwinup, Grant: "Walking" — *Harper's Bazaar* (October 1973)

Hass, F.J. and Dolan, E.F.: *The Foot Book* — Henry Regnery Company, Chicago (1973)

Haultrain, Arnold: *Of Walks and Walking Tours* — T. Werner Laurie Ltd., London (1914)

Hillaby, John: *Journey Through Britain* — Granada Publishing, London (1970)

Hillaby, John: *Journey Through Europe* — Granada Publishing, London (1974)

Hinrichsen, Gerda: *The Body Shop* — Taplinger Publishing Co., New York (1974)

Howarth, M.B.: "The Art and Technique of Walking" — *Consumer Bulletin* (April 1973)

Kauth, Benjamin: *Walk and Be Happy* — The John Day Co., New York (1960)

Keith, Arthur: *The Engines of the Human Body* — J.B. Lippincott Company, London (1920)

Klenerman, Leslie: *The Foot and Its Disorders* — Blackwell Scientific Publications, Oxford (1976)

Kraus, H., Rabb, W. and White, P.: *Hypokinetic Disease* — Charles C. Thomas Publishers, Springfield, Ill. (1961)

Larson, L.A. and Michelman, H.: *International Guidelines to Fitness and Health* — Crown Publishers, New York (1973)

Lindblom, K.G.: *The Use of Stilts* — Broderna Lagerstrom, Stockholm (1978)

Lucas, John A.: "Pedestrianism and the Struggle for the Sir John Astley Belt, 1878, 1879" — *Research Quarterly* (1968)

Margaria, Rodolpho: *Biomechanics and Energetics of Muscular Exercise* — Clarendon Press, Oxford (1976)

Marsden, J.P. and Montgomery, S.R.: "A General Survey of the Walking Habits of Individuals" — *Ergonomics* (1972)

Morehouse, L. and Miller, A.: *Physiology of Exercise* — The C.U. Mosby Company, St. Louis (1976)

Morris, Desmond: *Intimate Behaviour* — Random House, New York (1971)

Morris, Desmond: *Manwatching* — H.N. Abrams Inc., New York (1977)

Morton, D.J.: *Human Locomotion and Body Form* — Williams and Wilkins Company, Baltimore (1952)

Murray, M.P.: "Gait as a Total Pattern of Movement" — *American Journal of Physical Medicine* (1967)

Murray, M.P., Kory, R.C., Clarkson, B.H., and Sepic, S.B.: "Comparisons of Free and Fast Walking Patterns of Normal Men" — *American Journal of Physical Medicine* (1966)

Napier, John: "The Antiquity of Human Walking" — *Scientific American* (April 1967)

Norfolk, Donald: *The Habits of Health* — Avon Books, New York (1978)

Passmore, R. and Durnin, J.: *Energy, Work and Leisure* — Heinemann (Educational Books) Ltd., London (1967)

Peary, Robert E.: *The North Pole* — Hodder and Stoughton, London (1910)

Pignatelli, Princess Luciana: *The Beautiful People's Beauty Book* — The McCall Publishing Company, New York (1970)

Pollock, M., Dimmick, J., Miller, H., Kendrick, Z. and Linnerud, A.: "Effects of Mode of Training on Cardiovascular Function and Body Composition of Middle-aged Men" — *Medicine and Science in Sports* (1975)

Pollock, M., Miller, H., Janeway, R., Linnerud, A., Robertson, B. and Valentino, R.: "Effects of Walking on Body Composition and Cardiovascular Functions of Middle-aged Men" — *Journal of Applied Physiology* (January 1971)

President's Council on Physical Fitness and Sports: *National Adult Fitness Survey* — Washington (May 1973)

Ramsden, Florence: *Foot Comfort and Efficiency* — Thorsons Publishers, London

Roberts, Elizabeth: *On Your Feet* — Rodale Press, Emmaus, Pennsylvania (1975)

Rudner, Ruth: *Wandering* — The Dial Press, New York (1972)

Saunders, J., Inman, V. and Eberhart, H.: "Determinants In Normal and Pathological Gait," — *The Journal of Bone and Joint Surgery* (July 1953)

Sheehan, George: *Dr. Sheehan on Running* — Bantam Books, New York (1978)

Shephard, Roy: *Endurance Fitness* — University of Toronto Press, Toronto (1967)

Subotnick, Steven: *Podiatric Sports Medicine* — Futura Publishing, Mount Kisco, N.Y. (1975)

Surtees, Robert S.: *Mr. Sponge's Sporting Tour* — Bradbury, Agnew & Co., London (1852)

Sussman, Aaron and Goode, Ruth: *The Magic of Walking* — Simon and Schuster, New York (1967)

Thoreau, Henry: *The Writings of Henry David Thoreau* — Houghton Mifflin Company, New York (1906)

Toffler, Alvin: *Future Shock* — Random House, New York (1970)

Various (Anthology): *The Footpath Way* — Sidgwick and Jackson Ltd., London (1911)

Veblen, Thorstein: *Theory of the Leisure Class* — Modern Library, New York (1931)

Wells, K.F.: *Kinesiology* — Saunders, Philadelphia (1976)

Zochert, Donald (Ed.): *Walking in America* — Alfred A. Knopf, New York (1974)

GERALD DONALDSON estimates that he has already covered more than 50,000 miles on foot in places as far-flung as the Mexican Plateau, the Yorkshire dales, the Alps, the Canadian Prairies, the mountains of Wales, California beaches, the sidewalks of New York and the streets of Toronto, the city in which he lives.

While avidly pursuing walking as a way of life, Gerald Donaldson has written magazine articles and advertising copy, and is co-author with Leslie Michener of *The Exercise Book*.